Creating Culturally Affirming and Meaningful Assignments

Creating Culturally Affirming and Meaningful Assignments offers principles, strategies, and examples to aid in the development of inclusive college coursework in which all students feel seen and valued.

This resource prepares instructors to proactively consider ways to honor and engage with students' varied identities and lived experiences through assignments. Chapters cover the course design process, methods on getting to know your students, assignment options beyond the exam, and more. Reflection questions at the end of each chapter serve as a springboard for faculty and leadership conversations on equitable and inclusive teaching practices, while the Appendix features 20 example assignments sourced from various higher education disciplines.

An accessible, practical read, this guidebook is for any higher education instructor who wants to reimagine their assignments to center and celebrate students' varied cultural backgrounds and experiences.

Christine Harrington is a professor in the Department of Advanced Studies, Leadership, and Policy at Morgan State University, Baltimore, MD. As an expert in teaching and learning and student success, she has authored numerous acclaimed books and is frequently invited to present at colleges and universities.

This book helps instructors get down to business, truly operationalizing inclusive teaching. Building on foundational pedagogical pillars, chapters infuse cultural sensitivity into tried-and-true methods while pushing educators to consider novel equitable alternatives. A bounty of pragmatic solutions to meet a long-standing need.
Regan A. R. Gurung, Associate Vice Provost and Executive Director, Center for Teaching and Learning, Oregon State University

This edited volume is highly practical, focused, and valuable for today's equity-minded educators. Establishing a definition and the importance of culturally affirming and meaningful assignments, this collection provides specific guidelines for creating these tasks with discipline-specific and discipline-agnostic examples.
Flower Darby, Associate Director of the Teaching for Learning Center, University of Missouri

From beginning to end, this book centers students and their lived experiences as a necessary component for student success. The authors do an excellent job of providing readers with research, resources, and guidance to incorporate their students' experiences into the classroom through culturally affirming assignments.
Paul Hernandez, Senior Advisor to the President at Achieving the Dream

This book is an excellent teaching resource for new and seasoned faculty who want to engage their students through inclusive assignments. Faculty will find the numerous practical strategies and assignment examples helpful in this must-have resource as they develop their assignments.
Linda Garcia, Executive Director of the Center for Community College Student Engagement (CCSSE) at the University of Texas at Austin

This book focuses on what students want—and deserve: meaningful assignments that are inclusive of the range of experiences and backgrounds they bring to a course. Instructors are eager for guidance on examining and creating such assignments. This is the book we need for engaging in this important work.
Ellen Hernandez, Retired English Professor, Camden County College

Creating Culturally Affirming and Meaningful Assignments

A Practical Resource for Higher Education Faculty

Edited by
Christine Harrington

NEW YORK AND LONDON

Designed cover image: © Getty Images, #1438179130 shapecharge

First published 2024
by Routledge
605 Third Avenue, New York, NY 10158

and by Routledge
4 Park Square, Milton Park, Abingdon, Oxon OX14 4RN

Routledge is an imprint of the Taylor & Francis Group, an informa business

© 2024 Taylor & Francis

The right of Christine Harrington to be identified as the author of the editorial material, and of the authors for their individual chapters, has been asserted in accordance with sections 77 and 78 of the Copyright, Designs and Patents Act 1988.

All rights reserved. No part of this book may be reprinted or reproduced or utilised in any form or by any electronic, mechanical, or other means, now known or hereafter invented, including photocopying and recording, or in any information storage or retrieval system, without permission in writing from the publishers.

Trademark notice: Product or corporate names may be trademarks or registered trademarks, and are used only for identification and explanation without intent to infringe.

ISBN: 978-1-032-58130-9 (hbk)
ISBN: 978-1-032-58153-8 (pbk)
ISBN: 978-1-003-44379-7 (ebk)

DOI: 10.4324/9781003443797

Typeset in Optima
by Taylor & Francis Books

To my mom who was the most affirming person I have ever known.

Contents

List of contributors ix
Foreword xi
TIA BROWN MCNAIR
Acknowledgements xiii

Introduction 1
CHRISTINE HARRINGTON

1 Why Culturally Affirming and Meaningful Assignments Matter and the Course Design Process 7
CARLOS MORALES AND MAYRA OLIVARES-URUETA

2 What Makes Assignments Culturally Affirmative? 22
ADRIAN D. MARTIN

3 What Makes Assignments Meaningful? 37
BRIDGET AREND AND ERIKA R. CARLSON

4 Getting to Know Your Students: A First Step in Creating Culturally Affirming and Meaningful Assignments 54
SHANTELL STRICKLAND-DAVIS AND JAIRO MCMICAN

5 Exploring Assignment Options beyond the Exam 71
JAMES K. WINFIELD

6 Giving Choice in Assignments 87
MYRA J. GEORGE AND JENNIFER E. THOMPSON

7 Being Transparent about Assignment Expectations 101
ELLEN WASSERMAN AND TADÉ AYENI

8 Providing Assignment Support and Feedback   114
   M. GENEVA MURRAY AND ROBERT SCAFE

   Appendix: Assignment Examples from the Field   133
      Getting to Know Your Students Assignments 133
         Exploring Support Needs via a Survey 133
            M. GENEVA MURRAY
         Your Story 136
            EMILY MURAI
         Personal Artifacts 137
            CAMILLE LOCKLEAR GOINS
         Create Your Own Pride Flag 139
            KELSIE POTTER
         Life Story 140
            SCOTT MATTINGLY AND NADIA BHUIYAN
      Science and Allied Health 141
         Reflections and Connections 141
            CARALYN ZEHNDER
         Exploring Favorite Foods 143
            JUDY C. K. CHAN
         Formal Letter to Elected Official 144
            SHALINI SRINIVASAN
         Culture and Healthcare 145
            FATHIA RICHARDSON AND KATHLEEN POLIMENI
      Arts and Humanities 146
         Empowering Ideas: Philosophy Dialogue Project 146
            WENDY OSTROFF
         Oral History Project 147
            MEREDITH MAY
         We Poems: Collective Voices Speak Individual Truths 149
            PORTIA SCOTT
         Who We Are: Memoir Reading, Writing and Sharing 150
            LORRAINE CELLA
         Exploring Fascism in Spain 152
            LUNDEN E. MACDONALD
         A Collaborative Diversity, Equity, Inclusion, and Access (DEIA) Student Poster 153
            MARIE-THERESE C. SULIT AND CHARLES ZOLA
      Education 154
         Identity and Intersectionality Personal and Leadership Reflection 154
            THERESA HAUG-BELVIN

Language History Project 156
LAURA ALVAREZ AND SARAH CAPITELLI
Reclaiming Numbers and Healing from White Supremacy Culture 157
DIANA RECOUVREUR
Community Portrait 159
BRIE MORETTINI
Books You Wish You Read 160
BRIAN KAYSER

Index 162

Contributors

Bridget Arend, Associate Director of Teaching and Learning, Metropolitan State University of Denver

Tadé Ayeni, Director of Leadership Education and Assistant Professor, Washington State University

Tia Brown McNair, Vice President for Diversity, Equity and Student Success and Executive Director for the Truth, Racial Healing and Transformation Campus Centers, American Association of Colleges and Universities

Erika R. Carlson, Senior Director for Data Strategy, New York Jobs CEO Council

Myra J. George, Director, Strategic Planning and Assessment at the University of North Carolina, Charlotte

Christine Harrington, Professor, Department of Advanced Studies, Leadership, and Policy, Morgan State University

Jairo McMican, Associate Director of Equity Initiatives, Achieving the Dream, Inc.

Adrian D. Martin, Associate Professor, Department of Teaching, Learning, and Literacy, New Jersey City University

Carlos Morales, President, TCC Connect Campus—Tarrant County College

M. Geneva Murray, Senior Associate Director for Teaching, Center for Faculty Excellence, University of Oklahoma

Mayra Olivares-Urueta, Executive in Residence, University of North Texas

Robert Scafe, Professional Development Specialist, Center for Faculty Excellence and Director, Writing Enriched Curriculum, University of Oklahoma

Shantell Strickland-Davis, Associate Vice President, Organizational Learning and Leadership Development at Central Piedmont Community College, Charlotte, NC

Jennifer E. Thompson, English Adjunct Lecturer, Borough of Manhattan Community College

Ellen Wasserman, Research Associate, Community College Research Center, Teachers College, Columbia University

James K. Winfield, Associate Dean for First Year Experience, General Education, and Retention Strategies, Southern New Hampshire University

Foreword

Tia Brown McNair

Everyone has a story, and that story influences the ways in which we engage with others and our environments. As educators, who we are and our funds of knowledge shape how we design our courses and assignments to promote student engagement, learning, diversity of ideas, and success. The same is true for our students. Their lived experiences are valuable assets to creating learning environments where they can thrive and belong. So, for those of us who understand the importance of these concepts to student success, this book, *Creating Culturally Affirming and Meaningful Assignments*, will provide important reminders of why student identity should remain at the heart of our work. For those of you who are reading this book because you want to learn more about designing assignments that advance equity and embrace diversity, the practical guidance offered will start you on that journey.

I remember my first teaching assignment as a graduate student pursuing my master's degree in English. Like many of you, I was handed the prepared syllabus for a first-year English composition course that was developed by my faculty mentor, and my job was to follow the course as it was designed. The first class was supposed to be simple. Do brief introductions, go over the syllabus and the course requirements, and assign the first writing assignment. The first assignment wasn't focused on getting to know my students. It jumped right into the content for the course because, as I was told, we had a limited amount of time to cover the required topics. That was a mistake. I know that now. I should have asked the students to write a personal narrative, so I could get to know them, what motivated them, and what they wanted from the course. I should have shared my journey with them. I was only five years older than many of them in the class. When I was explaining the syllabus, I should have connected the course content and learning outcomes to the skill sets and competencies associated with their academic and social mobility. In other words, I should have explained why this course mattered and why I was invested in their success.

> At the American Association of Colleges and Universities, our work is grounded in equity and inclusion, [and] our vision of educational excellence is focused on the learning all students need for success in an uncertain future and for addressing the compelling issues we face as a democracy and as a global community—regardless of where they study, what they major in, or what their career goals may be.
> (AAC&U n.d.)

For many years, we have advocated for the practices outlined in this book as foundations for excellence and student success; inclusive learning environments that embrace student diversity, transparency, defined learning outcomes, formative assessments of learning, giving choice in assignments, and meaningful experiences that encourage applied learning (i.e., high-impact practices). At a time when the value of student diversity and identity are being challenged as core to educational design, we must remain true to the teaching and learning strategies that we know are fundamental for the success of all students. Our journey is challenging, now more so than ever, but we will prevail because we are focused on what has always mattered—students.

Reference

AAC&U (n.d.). About AAC&U. www.aacu.org/about.

Acknowledgements

As this was my first experience editing a book, I am so grateful to the colleagues who were willing to collaborate with me on this project. I am so appreciative of all the chapter authors and example contributors who shared their time, expertise, and diverse perspectives. Collectively, we created an important resource that will support faculty as they strive to create culturally affirming and meaningful assignments. I enjoyed the lively and collaborative conversations we had via author meetings and email exchanges. The ideas and feedback you shared along the way added tremendous value to this project. I have learned so much from all of you and was truly honored to be able to lead this effort and work with so many talented, amazing educators who are so committed to creating more equitable learning paths and environments.

A special thank you to all of you who have invited me to speak at your college, university, or conference. Through these opportunities, I heard from faculty about their needs, and this was one source of inspiration for this book. I am always energized by virtual and in-person professional development.

I am also grateful to John von Knorring, who believed in the need for this book, and for his initial guidance as I mapped out a plan. Thank you also to Alex Andrews at Routledge for his support during the editorial processes.

I would also like to thank my family, friends, and colleagues who continually provide me with support and encouragement. My husband, two sons Ryan and David, my niece Ashley, her husband Glen, and their two daughters Ariella and Isabella, and my father not only support me with all that I do, including my hobby of writing books for faculty, but perhaps more importantly remind me of the importance of work–life balance. I am so fortunate to be surrounded by love and family members and friends who bring me so much joy.

Thank you to the chapter authors: Bridget Arend, Tadé Ayeni, Erika R. Carlson, Myra J. George, Jairo McMican, Adrian D. Martin, Carlos Morales, M. Geneva Murray, Mayra Olivares-Urueta, Robert Scafe, Shantell Strickland-Davis, Jennifer E. Thompson, Ellen Wasserman, and James K.

Winfield. Thank you also to the example contributors: Laura Alvarez, Nadia Bhuiyan, Sarah Capitelli, Judy C. K. Chan, Lorraine Cella, Theresa Haug-Belvin, Brian Kayser, Camille Locklear Goins, Lunden E. MacDonald, Scott Mattingly, Meredith May, Brie Morettini, Emily Murai, M. Geneva Murray, Wendy L. Ostroff, Kathleen Polimeni, Kelsie Potter, Diana Recouvreur, Fathia Richardson, Portia Scott, Shalini Srinivasan, Marie-Therese C. Sulit, Caralyn Zehnder, and Charles Zola. Thank you also to Delnita Evans for her assistance with the index.

Introduction

Christine Harrington

Colleges and universities across the country have been focusing on ways to improve student success outcomes, especially for Black, Latine (a gender-inclusive term that is more consistent with Spanish grammar), and other historically marginalized students. One of the most important ways to increase retention and improve graduation rates is by creating inclusive classroom learning experiences where all students feel valued and develop a sense of belonging. There have been numerous books and resources published and professional development events offered that were designed to support instructors in creating inclusive learning environments, yet there has been very little instructor support specifically targeting assignments.

Why a Book on Assignments?

Assignments are a critical part of a student's educational journey. As discussed by Winfield (Chapter 5), traditional assignments such as exams and research papers can perpetuate equity gaps as these types of assignments are often biased, activate stereotype threat in students, and are not based on or representative of diverse perspectives. Too often students are in learning environments where the perspectives and ideas shared predominantly represent privileged groups such as White males while the voices and perspectives of others are missing or marginalized. Traditional assignments can leave many students not feeling affirmed culturally and this may lead to students not developing the strong sense of belonging that is so critical to their success.

In many cases, traditional assignments do not mirror the skills that graduates will need to demonstrate in the world of work and are therefore not perceived as meaningful by students (see Chapter 3). Most employers will not ask their employees to take an exam or write a 20-page research paper as part of their job duties. Students may struggle to see the value of assignments that do not connect to their personal and professional lives.

DOI: 10.4324/9781003443797-1

In my latest book, *Keeping Us Engaged: Student Perspectives (and Research Evidence) on What Works and Why* (Harrington, 2021), I invited students from colleges and universities across the country to share what their faculty did to engage them. An overwhelming number of the students' stories focused on assignments. Students viewed assignments as an essential part of their college experience and appreciated having meaningful assignments that had clear instructions, connected to their lived experiences, and aligned with their goals. Students also valued having assignment choices, noting that this gave them more ownership over their learning experience.

As I shared the students' stories at professional development presentations I gave at colleges and universities across the nation, I found that instructors were very interested in learning more about how to improve their assignments so that students found them more valuable and engaging. The need for a resource specifically focused on assignments became apparent.

As I wanted this resource to benefit all students, especially students who have historically been less likely to earn credentials and degrees because practices in higher education are inequitable, I knew it was important to focus explicitly on inclusive teaching practices. Many current professional development resources have a cultural focus using terms such as "culturally responsive" and "culturally relevant" practices, but I wanted to go a step further and intentionally chose to use the term "culturally affirming." I wanted to develop a resource that challenged instructors to proactively consider ways to honor and value students' varied identities and lived experiences through assignments. As Martin writes in Chapter 2, "Culturally affirming assignments are learning tasks, endeavors, and exercises that reflect a value for students' cultural identities, acknowledge how content and learning processes are culturally constructed, and uphold cultural diversity as a productive, meaningful, and generative learning asset."

I invited a diverse group of practitioner–scholars to author chapters and share assignment examples, and I am so thankful for their expertise and contributions. Based on the collective work presented in this book and my own scholarship, I have created a Culturally Affirming and Meaningful Checklist that can be used as a resource when instructors consider how to create culturally affirming and meaningful assignments and evaluate and revise current assignments. It is hoped that instructors at colleges and universities across the nation apply the principles and use the strategies described in this book to create affirming and meaningful assignments and that, as a result of these actions, all students have a stronger sense of belonging and higher levels of achievement.

Culturally Affirming and Meaningful Assignments Checklist

This checklist was designed to be used as a reflective resource for instructors striving to create culturally affirming and meaningful assignments. Not all items will apply to every class or every assignment; instructors need to determine what is appropriate for their course and discipline. The checklist is not intended to be scored or used quantitatively, but rather as a self-assessment tool to help instructors create or revise assignments so that they are perceived as affirming and valuable by students.

Initial Considerations

1. Have you reflected on how your positionality, beliefs, values, and experiences may influence what types of assignments you require and how campus professionals and colleagues can help you design or redesign assignments that are culturally affirming and meaningful?
2. Did you consider alternatives to traditional summative assignments that allow students to demonstrate learning in creative and personally relevant ways? Did you identify formative assignments that will help students know if they are on track for success?
3. Did you learn about your students before the start of the semester and use this information to determine assignments?
4. Did you reflect on what assumptions you may be making about students' prior knowledge and what assignment support may benefit students?

Assignment Design

1. Will the assignment (and assignment choices, if given) enable students to demonstrate that they achieved the learning outcomes of the course and program?
2. Does the assignment allow students to demonstrate their learning in diverse ways?
3. Does the assignment build on and value of students' prior knowledge and experiences?
4. Will the assignment help students develop a multicultural orientation or perspective?
5. Does the assignment provide an opportunity for students to engage with and learn from others?
6. Does the assignment require students to make connections between what they are learning and their personal and professional lives?
7. Do the skills learned via the assignment have immediate and future real-world value?
8. Do you allow students to choose the topic and/or sources for assignments? If so, what guidance do you provide to help students decide on a topic?
9. Do you allow students to make process choices such as working independently or in a group or determining due dates?
10. Is the assignment at the "just-right" level of challenge? How do you know?

Transparent Communication of Assignment

1 Have you communicated how the assignment links to course learning outcomes and career skills?
2 Is the purpose of the assignment communicated?
3 Is a sequential list of the steps or tasks students need to take to complete the assignment successfully provided?
4 Did you use easy-to-understand, jargon-free language to communicate assignment expectations?
5 Did you share examples or models that illustrate various ways students can complete the assignment?
6 Did you communicate grading criteria and scheme, how assignment feedback would be provided, and if opportunities such as revise and resubmit options or reflective assignment components to use feedback immediately are available?

Overview of the Book

There are eight chapters in this book and an appendix comprised of assignment examples from the field. Each chapter begins with a story and then provides research-based strategies related to the chapter topic. Instructors will find reflection questions at the end of each chapter. Instructors are encouraged to use these questions to prompt discussions with colleagues, perhaps through book group discussions.

In Chapter 1, Morales and Olivares-Urueta provide historical context for why instructors need to invest time and energy into revising or reimagining assignments so that students find them culturally affirming and meaningful. They also provide readers with foundational knowledge about how instructor positionality influences the course design process and the backward design and ADDIE models of instructional design so that instructors can see how creating assignments fits into the overall course design process. Finally, they suggest ways in which instructors can share the course design and assignment expectations in the syllabus.

In Chapter 2, Martin defines what is meant by culturally affirming assignments. In doing so, he introduces five principles that instructors can use as a guide when creating culturally affirming assignments. These principles are as follows: valuing students' cultural identities; acknowledging the ways culture informs content and learning processes; upholding multiculturalism as a learning asset; supporting relational engagement with students; and offering diverse ways for students to demonstrate their learning.

In Chapter 3, Arend and Carlson describe what makes assignments meaningful. They offer five guiding principles for instructors aiming to make their assignments more meaningful to students. They believe that meaningful assignments are aligned with learning outcomes, personally relevant and culturally affirming, challenging, empowering and growth-focused, authentic, with real-world value, and skill-based and relevant to the world of work.

Instructors will discover how getting to know students is an essential first step in creating culturally affirming and meaningful assignments in Chapter 4. In this chapter, Strickland-Davis and McMican explain the role of relationships in learning and provide instructors with numerous strategies that they can use to get to know students before the semester begins and early in the semester. They also provide strategies instructors can use to nurture these relationships throughout the semester.

In Chapter 5, Winfield discusses equity concerns associated with traditional assignments such as exams and research papers, and encourages instructors to identify innovative summative assignments that students will find affirming and meaningful. He shares examples such as infographics, one-pagers or executive summaries, Pecha Kucha presentations, podcasts, videos, social media posts or blogs, book reviews, experiential learning assignments, and training manuals. He also suggests that instructors incorporate numerous formative assessments into their course design so students, and their instructors, know if they are on track to meet with success in the course.

In Chapter 6, George and Thompson explain the value of choice and the importance of ensuring all assignment options will demonstrate evidence of learning outcomes. They provide numerous suggestions on how instructors can give students content, product, and process assignment choices. They argue that it is difficult for an assignment to be culturally affirming and meaningful to all students and thus choices are needed. George and Thompson discuss how choice helps students take more ownership of their learning experience and how choice increases the likelihood that students will find the assignment experience affirming and valuable.

In Chapter 7, Wasserman and Ayeni discuss the importance of transparent assignments from an equity perspective. They note that all students, but especially first-generation students, students of color, and others from marginalized groups, benefit from clearly stated assignment expectations. In addition, they explain that being transparent means clearly communicating the purpose, tasks, and grading criteria for all assignments.

In Chapter 8, Murray and Scafe focus on the importance of providing support to students while they work on their assignments and of high-quality feedback on assignments. They challenge instructors to consider not only the assumptions they may make about students' prior knowledge but also how they might provide scaffolded support and examples, increase formative assessment opportunities, and connect students to resources, if needed. They provide an overview of the characteristics of useful instructor feedback and provide suggestions on how to help students give quality peer feedback.

The Appendix consists of assignment examples from the field. Twenty instructors teaching at various institutions provide examples of assignments and share why students will find these culturally affirming and meaningful. Several getting-to-know-you assignments that can be easily adapted to different courses in various disciplines and examples from the STEM and allied health, arts and humanities, and education fields are shared.

Reference

Harrington, C. (2021). *Keeping us engaged: Student perspectives (and research evidence) on what works and why*. Routledge.

Chapter 1

Why Culturally Affirming and Meaningful Assignments Matter and the Course Design Process

Carlos Morales and Mayra Olivares-Urueta

It had been almost a decade since I (Mayra) last taught, but this time I was going into the classroom full-time with years of experience as a college administrator. I had seen a lot in 16 years as a student affairs professional, having served in an executive role at a community college during the pandemic while working from home with a four-year-old and a six-year-old. Prior to that, I had earned a Ph.D. after having successfully migrated from Mexico with my widowed mother, sister, and grandmother. I survived ESL, developmental math, and English, and graduated out of government assistance (all the attributes and experiences that deemed me a student "at-risk"). Yet, stepping into a classroom to teach was terrifying. I was handed a ready-made syllabus and accompanying texts. As I reviewed the materials, I prayed I would not butcher any of them. Moreover, I hoped my students would not sense my nervousness and the presence of imposter syndrome which often visited me while I was being watched by many expectant faces. And then a few months in … it clicked. I let my fear go and trusted myself and my lived experience, as my partner had suggested. I started engaging more meaningfully with the materials, connecting assignments to my lived experiences, creating case studies out of those experiences, and helping students dig deep into themselves to connect meaningfully with the material. I knew I wanted my students to come out with pragmatic knowledge that they would be able to apply to their careers. To that end, I changed a major assignment for one of the classes because it just "felt" better, and more meaningful.

This journey represents my haphazard arrival at course design and culturally affirming teaching. This happened after reading some books and attending a few professional development courses, but it could have been better. It is hoped that this chapter and book will provide the tools and strategies to enable instructors to apply culturally affirming course design meaningfully and naturally.

Creating culturally affirming and reflective assignments using Martin's principles (see Chapter 2) requires more than a formula or template; it requires a willingness by individual instructors to know about the

DOI: 10.4324/9781003443797-2

educational system, the inequities therein, and how these inequities can show up (or not) in our classrooms via curriculum design and implementation (Riback, 2021). Moreover, instructors must acknowledge that differential outcomes in the success of minoritized and historically excluded student populations are not due to student ability (Sensoy & DiAngelo, 2017). Inquisitiveness about what, outside of the student, perpetuates these inequities is a must for instructors who want to be culturally affirming in their classrooms. Culture is often seen as tied to race, so throughout this chapter race will be discussed as a major factor impacting culture in classrooms and curricula. Zaretta Hammond has highlighted that educators must be aware of themselves as people who live in a racialized country with racialized educational systems and how race impacts not only their interactions and activities but also their engagement in the classroom with their students, the curriculum, and the educational system (Riback, 2021a).

Historical Context

A succinct historical context can contextualize the work that instructors will need to do to create culturally affirming and meaningful assignments. According to Thelin (2019), from their inception, colleges and universities in the United States were created with the purpose of serving wealthy White men. Moreover, universities were used as places in which Indigenous people would be assimilated into the culture of the new European immigrants who were suddenly in charge. Universities were used to spread Anglo-European ideals, morals, and culture. This assimilation and indoctrination into U.S. ideals and society, as set by White, Christian, high-class ideals, has historically been one of the main goals of our educational system.

Thelin (2019) reminded us that from colonial times, higher education institutions were the source of the clergy and political leaders of their time. Cities were intentional in the establishment of universities as it was noted they trained the people who would become leaders of the businesses and religious and civic organizations of the cities in which they were housed. As the country developed, so too did the universities, their populations, and their fields of study. In the 1800s, medical and law degrees became part of the higher education landscape, and it was no longer just wealthy men but also some of the middle-class and high-class aspiring families who were sending their sons, predominantly, to college to become business and community leaders (Thelin, 2019). As emancipation was slowly rolled out in the country and the great migration got underway, so too was the establishment of schools for Black people and by Black people (Johnson, 2020). Harmon (2012, p. 17) noted that newly freed African Americans had a great desire for learning how to read and write, which did not dissipate as time went on. Literacy was extremely important as it brought the assurance of emancipation. Emancipation was and is the freedom to think for oneself.

The second Morrill Act was established in part to fund higher education opportunities for African Americans through the creation of agricultural and technical colleges which were to be exclusively for their enrollment. These educational opportunities did not materialize as intended as college leaders decided to use funds for the benefit and enhancement of already established programs for White students (Thelin, 2019). Nonetheless, higher education began to morph as newly freed Blacks entered it. The doors did not open in any substantial way for African Americans in higher education until Historically Black Colleges and Universities (HBCUs) emerged in the latter part of the nineteenth century (Giles, 2006). Just as universities were the training grounds for White leadership in the United States, "Black colleges offered special sanctuaries of learning and development to prepare other leaders for the Black community" (Giles, 2006, p. 106). Prominent leaders such as Dr. Martin Luther King Jr., Dr. Howard Thurman, and Maynard Jackson—the first Black mayor of Atlanta—all graduated from HBCUs. Giles (2006, p. 114) quoted Dr. Thurman reflecting on the self-love and respect he had for himself as a result of attending Morehouse College:

> [College president Dr. Hope] addressed us as young gentlemen. What this term of respect meant to our faltering ego can only be understood against the backdrop of the South of the 1920s. We were Black men in Atlanta during a period when the state of Georgia was infamous for its brutality [toward Black people].

Thus, aside from providing alternative higher education opportunities for Black Americans, HBCUs were also places of respite in an incessantly hostile world.

Indigenous populations had their own tumultuous history and engagement with higher education institutions. Aside from what has already been noted, Indigenous people in the United States endured forced education through boarding schools. These schools were created specifically for Indigenous people and the goal was to "kill the Indian, save the man" (Howe, 2016), meaning the aim was to "civilize" Indigenous children and make them more European in all realms of life—religious practice, attire and looks, education, and so forth. After many decades as centers of cultural genocide, boarding schools experienced their own transformation and became Indigenous-run in the middle of the twentieth century. This transformation meant that tribes were now in charge of the schools and the curricula. Moreover, because many of the people who were teaching in and leading the schools had attended native boarding schools themselves, they made sure their horrible experiences were not perpetuated now that they were in control (Howe, 2016). Another important educational change happened in the late 1960s through the creation of Tribal Colleges. A report by the American Indian Higher Education Consortium stated Tribal Colleges were created in part to provide higher education options for tribal citizens specifically in geographically isolated areas of the country (American Indian Higher Education Consortium and Institute for Higher Education Policy, 1999). The Tribal Colleges have become cultural epicenters in their communities, bringing higher education opportunities to the tribal citizens, creating opportunities for growth through the provision of GED and other community-advancing options, and generating leaders for the communities. Like HBCUs, part of the success and draw of students to Tribal Colleges come from the fact they are staffed by community tribal members who care for the students as if they were family. Tribal culture is validated and supported in the colleges through the teaching of Indigenous languages and by employing tribal members who intentionally teach about Indigenous culture in culturally affirming and asset-based ways (Howe, 2016; American Indian Higher Education Consortium and Institute for Higher Education Policy, 1999).

Although Latinx communities do not have the equivalent of HBCUs or Tribal Colleges, there are Hispanic Serving Institutions (HSIs). Higher education institutions are designated HSIs (after an application process and evaluation) if at least 25 percent of their enrolled students self-identify as Hispanic (Hispanic Association of Colleges and Universities, n.d.). The major difference between HSIs, HBCUs, and Tribal Colleges is that HSIs are still often predominantly White institutions. The cultural component embedded in HBCUs and Tribal Colleges is not naturally part of HSIs and thus leaves the opportunity for cultural reflectivity and intentional validation.

This condensed history of higher education, including some of our minority-serving institutions (HBCUs, Tribal Colleges, and HSIs), sets the stage for the why of culturally affirming teaching. Although higher education institutions have been around for hundreds of years in the United States, they have not been inclusive and reflective of the diversity of people in this country. Aside from the exclusion in participation and enrollment, the curriculum has not traditionally included perspectives of minoritized populations. Leaders who helped establish Tribal Colleges and HBCUs and identify HSIs and Asian American- and Native American Pacific Islander-serving institutions have done so in part to provide settings in which students are seen as opportunity- and asset-filled rather than as people who require fixing and assimilation. While there is still much work to do to make higher education truly reflective of our communities, this book should be a step in the right direction in helping instructors understand why culturally affirming assignments matter and how they can begin to incorporate them into any discipline. All curricula and assignments can be culturally affirming.

Instructor Positionality and Course Design

Identity matters, and as instructors seek to reach more students and create educational environments that are more culturally affirming, it is vital that instructors understand their positionality. As Kezar (2002, p. 96) pointed out, "Within positionality theory, it is acknowledged that people have multiple overlapping identities. Thus, people make meaning from various aspects of their identity including social class." Harrington (2022) advocated for instructors to consider their positionality just as researchers are encouraged to do. In the following paragraphs, the authors describe their positionalities as they permeate every aspect of their work as scholars–practitioners–faculty members.

Mayra Olivares-Urueta's Positionality

As much as I tried to fit into the ideals of what higher education leadership looked like, it was impossible to fit into those ideals. Higher education remains a place where leadership inside and outside the classroom is still predominantly White and male. I found myself trying to fit into the dominant groups' identity and culture. The shoe did not fit because that is not who I am. I am a Mexican-American immigrant who completed English as a second language and developmental courses. I grew up in a lower-middle-class home whose head of household was a widowed Mexican immigrant. I am a mother, a wife, bilingual and bicultural, cisgender and heterosexual. Ironically, the role in which I settled into my positionality, my intersecting identities, was as vice president for student affairs. I found that wearing the shoe that fit me best—being authentically myself—enabled me to be the best vice president I could be.

Imposter syndrome lurks, though. Even though I embrace my positionality and see the benefits of being authentically myself everywhere, especially in my classroom, I must constantly affirm and validate my work. Imposter syndrome is real and can shake me up even on my best days. This doubt in myself and my ability has roots in the historical underpinnings of our higher education system, and even the establishment of the United States. People in minoritized communities are socialized to be subjugated and believe we are lesser than the powerful majority. Learning to undo this harm takes time, and one of the ways it manifests itself in daily life is imposter syndrome. Owning my worth and value and tuning out the little imposter syndrome monsters is a daily practice.

Still, I have found that leaning into who I am—my positionality—has made me a more effective teacher. Furthermore, it has freed my students to be authentic themselves. Students have shared deeply personal stories about who they are and why it matters in my courses and through assignments. Creating a context and an environment where I am authentically myself has opened the door for assignments and coursework in which I invite students to bring themselves and their culture into our studies. Just as I have done with my students, I want to invite instructors to seriously consider their identities and how they influence their positionality in the classroom. Instructors can ask themselves:

- What have I already put out into the universe?
- What have I tucked away and why?
- How can I bring out this identity and celebrate it?
- What role does imposter syndrome play in my ability to be my authentic self in my classroom?
- Am I naming imposter syndrome and actively discussing it with my students so they may acknowledge and fight it together?

When instructors show up to their classrooms as their most authentic selves, they are opening the door for their students to do the same. The results can be magical and extremely validating for students.

Carlos Morales's Positionality

As a scientist with a background in biology and microbiology, I celebrate positionality and the role it plays in higher education classrooms. For me, education is the path toward a better life where individuals can grow and develop. Education facilitates socioeconomic mobility and fosters citizenship. My educator life started in Puerto Rico, where the society, while diverse, is more homogeneous than in the United States due to it being an island. There are three races in Puerto Rico: Taíno Indians, African Slaves, and Spaniards. Our culture is rich in the three ethnicities and this richness has shaped the way I relate to people from other locations and cultures. In my case, my family is "biracial" (a term I am reluctant to use because it is not generally used in my culture): my dad is White and my mom is light Black. I have two younger sisters: the older one is fair-skinned, blonde, and has green eyes; the younger one is caramel-skinned and has black hair and brown eyes. I grew up in a middle-class family: my dad went to college and became a civil engineer and land surveyor; my mother went to college and obtained an associate's degree; and my younger sister obtained a master's degree in electrical engineering. I have four cousins who went to college, too. As children, we always heard that we needed to go to college as it was an expectation. In my neighborhood, we were surrounded by other families where the head of the household—and in many cases both parents—went to college. We had access to teachers, lawyers, nurses, medical technologists, accountants, businesspeople, computer technicians, agronomists, social workers, and doctors. Many of my friends went to college and became professionals in many of the fields mentioned above.

As an educator, I have been in face-to-face and virtual classrooms for almost 30 years, teaching future scientists and educators. I have found myself advising them on the importance of education and the importance of continuing advanced studies as they share their backgrounds, frustrations, and the challenges they overcame to get to college. I have done this at two-year, four-year, and graduate levels in both public and private institutions, mostly Hispanic Serving Institutions (HSIs). I transitioned to administration about 20 years ago; however, I continued to teach. Currently, I am the founding president of the virtual campus of Tarrant County College—the largest of the six campuses and the only virtual campus in the state of Texas. By establishing a virtual campus, I have helped the institution increase access for students who want to attend college but face transportation, accessibility, and/or financial difficulties. Through my role, I invest and give back to the community as a facilitator of higher education attainment.

There have been instances where I have questioned my decisions and sometimes my abilities in all my roles—even though I have many years of experience. The imposter syndrome kicks in and, like many other individuals, I feel that sense of insecurity that shows up a few hours before presenting a new idea or big project. I have developed my own strategies to cope with these thoughts and continue producing for my students and colleagues.

Life, educational, and professional experiences play a paramount role in the design of assignments that are pertinent and valid and allow for real-life applications that transcend the classroom, independent of the modality being used to teach.

Instructional Design Approaches

Instructional design can be defined as the process instructors use to determine course learning outcomes, assessments, and teaching and learning strategies. The main goal is to ensure the quality of instruction and student learning. Through this process, instructors will continually revise the design and delivery of their courses to ensure students learn and achieve the goals of the course.

Using intentional course design processes can take significant instructor time and effort before the semester starts, and requires ongoing assessment and evaluation (Michael & Libarkin, 2016). Engaging in the course design process is a good investment, however, as student learning is higher when instructors design courses thoughtfully (Association for

Supervision and Curriculum Development, 2012). Research has shown that students are more engaged and learn more when courses are thoughtfully designed (Reynolds & Kearns, 2017; Swan et al., 2012). If instructors do not engage in instructional design, students may not walk away with the knowledge and understanding they need for success in future courses and their careers.

Designing courses can be challenging (Michael & Libarkin, 2016). Fortunately, most colleges and universities offer instructional design support. Instructors can tap into the expertise of instructional designers and teaching and learning center staff for support with the course design process. There are numerous instructional design models. Two of the most widely used—backward design and ADDIE—are discussed below.

Understanding by Design: A Backward Course Design Process

One of the most pivotal design frameworks, Understanding by Design (UbD), created by Wiggins and McTighe, is a backward design process (Association for Supervision and Curriculum Development, 2012). Wiggins and McTighe (2005) have challenged instructors to begin the process by identifying the big ideas of their courses. The UbD framework helps educators prioritize concepts and knowledge within the course, drawing the most attention to content that will serve students well in the future. In the UbD model, there are four types of learning goals: knowledge, skills, understanding, and long-term transfer goals. As so much knowledge is easily available, modern education should strive to prepare students for long-term transfer, to be able to apply learning to new situations.

Wiggins and McTighe (2005) have suggested that faculty should design their courses with the end in mind, using a three-stage backward design process. The first stage is identifying course learning outcomes; determining assessments that provide evidence of learning outcome achievement is the second stage; and planning activities or the teaching method that will best support students on this learning journey is the third stage.

Identifying Learning Outcomes

Beginning with the end in mind, the first stage of the backward design process involves instructors determining the course learning outcomes—or what they want students to know, think, or do by the end of the course. During this process, instructors need to consider how course goals align with program and institutional goals. Another important consideration during this stage is the transfer of knowledge to ensure that learning is long-lasting. As instructors grapple with what they want students to know, they need to specify the level of understanding or knowledge expected. According to the UbD framework, "when someone truly understands, they can explain, interpret, apply, demonstrate perspective, display empathy, and have self-knowledge and the ability to be reflective" (Association for Supervision and Curriculum Development, 2012, p. 5).

College instructors can use classifications and taxonomies of learning to think more strategically about the level of learning desired in their courses. The work of Bloom and Fink can be very helpful when determining course learning outcomes. Benjamin Bloom's taxonomy of the cognitive domain was developed by a team of scholars in the 1950s and revised in 2001 (Henning & Roberts, 2016). This taxonomy has been used by countless educators to design, structure, and assess learning. The six categories in Bloom's taxonomy for the cognitive domain are: remember, understand, apply, analyze, evaluate, and create (Henning & Roberts, 2016). Many online resources provide lists of action verbs related to each of the categories within Bloom's taxonomy to help instructors write measurable learning outcomes.

Another popular taxonomy for developing meaningful outcomes is the taxonomy of significant learning. Dee Fink, a student of Bloom, built upon Bloom's taxonomy and created a new taxonomy by interviewing not only educators but students about what they considered to be significant learning moments and significant kinds of learning (Henning & Roberts, 2016). Fink (2013) defined significant learning as learning that changes how a student lives their personal, social, civic, or professional life. Fink's (2013) taxonomy of significant learning has six categories: foundational knowledge, integration, application, human dimension, caring, and learning how to learn.

The foundational knowledge, integration, and application categories within Fink's taxonomy of significant learning framework are like those in Bloom's taxonomy in that they focus on cognitive skills: specifically, what students will be expected to know and how they will be expected to integrate and use the information learned (Henning & Roberts, 2016). The other three categories—human dimension, caring, and learning how to learn—are often referred to as the affective and reflective aspects of learning. The human dimension category focuses on what students need to understand or know about themselves and what kinds of capabilities they will need in terms of interacting with other people. In the caring category, the focus is on the values or interests that students have or will develop, while the learning how to learn dimension focuses on the capabilities students will need to learn more in the future. Instructors have welcomed Fink's (2013) taxonomy of significant learning because it emphasizes learning that extends beyond the end of the course. Instructors who use it are challenged to think about their hopes for their students in the future.

Determining Assessments

The second stage of the backward design process requires instructors to determine what assessment evidence is needed for students to demonstrate their achievement of the learning outcomes. This second stage—determining assessments or assignments—is the focus of this book. As Winfield (Chapter 5) points out, many different academic products, such as media projects, infographics, and presentations, can be used to illustrate what a student has learned. George and Thompson (Chapter 6) advocate that students should be allowed to choose how they demonstrate their achievement of the course learning outcomes. For example, in a language history project, Alvarez and Capitelli allow their students to choose the modality and offer suggested formats such as drawings, slideshows, poems, graphic novels or comic strips, children's books, collages, maps, timelines, videos, and podcasts (see Appendix, Example 17).

Determining Teaching Methods

The final stage of the UbD framework is the planning stage. During this stage, instructors identify the learning activities that will help students successfully demonstrate their achievement of the learning outcomes via the assigned assessments (Association for Supervision and Curriculum Development, 2012). Learning activities may include lectures, discussions, demonstrations, small group work, partner work, labs, and more. During this final stage, instructors determine how they can support student learning.

ADDIE

Another widely used instructional design model is ADDIE, which stands for Analysis, Design, Development, Implementation, and Evaluation (Reigeluth et al., 2016). The five-phased ADDIE process encourages instructors to consider numerous factors associated with the learning process and to view design as an ongoing process.

Analysis Phase

In the analysis phase, instructors ask themselves questions about their students and the learning environment. When faculty know about their students, it will be more likely that they will design culturally affirming courses (see Chapter 4). As instructors get to know their students, they want to discover what students hope to learn from the course, how they might prefer to learn it, and what supports they may need. M. Geneva Murray notes that she uses a survey assignment to gather this information (see Appendix, Example 1). It can also be important for instructors to assess students' comfort and ability with various learning modalities and tools (Woodley et al., 2017).

Design Phase

The design phase involves determining the course learning outcomes, types of assessments, and learning activities. To develop culturally affirming assignments, instructors can use what they learned in the analysis phase about students and the learning environment to craft assignments that are culturally affirming and meaningful. It is important that the assignment expectations are transparently communicated (see Chapter 7). During this design phase, instructors can also consider how much the assignment grade should count toward the final grade, given factors such as alignment to course learning outcomes and complexity, time, and effort needed.

Development Phase

During the development phase, the instructor applies the planning that took place during the design stage to develop the course. Although this process can vary based on course modality, most, if not all, courses have an online presence through a learning management system. As a result, this development stage typically involves inputting content into the learning management system. As content is being uploaded and packaged for students in the learning management system, it is important to review the functionality and applicability of technology components. When sharing the identified culturally affirming assignments, it can be helpful to connect these explicitly back to the course learning outcomes so students can easily see the relevance of each assignment (see Chapter 3). Likewise, instructors can make connections between the formative and summative assessments to help students see how all aspects of their learning journey fit together.

Implementation Phase

The learning experience is launched during the implementation phase. During this phase, it is important for instructors to show learners how to navigate the course and share what resources are available. As students complete formative assessments, the feedback that instructors provide will guide and support them during their learning journey. Murray and Scafe (Chapter 8) provide numerous strategies for providing useful feedback in a culturally affirming way.

Evaluation Phase

During the evaluation phase, instructors assess the effectiveness of the overall course design and implementation. This includes determining how well assignments worked. Collecting data on the utilization, alignment, and functionality of all the course components can be helpful for instructors as they reflect on what worked well and where improvements could be made. Engaging in this continuous improvement cycle enables instructors to make immediate adjustments as needed throughout the course and informs how they design subsequent course offerings.

Communicating Course Design via the Syllabus

The syllabus is another important way in which instructors can communicate course design to students. Moreover, it can be used to engage and motivate students (Harrington & Thomas, 2018). Students want to know what they will be learning, what will be expected of them, and how this course relates to their lives and goals. Through transparent communication on the syllabus, instructors can help students understand the type of work they will be doing and why it is important (see Chapter 7).

Often, instructors are required to use standardized syllabi templates provided by their institution, which may make it more challenging to set the tone for a culturally affirming learning environment. There are, however, opportunities for the instructor's voice, values, and classroom culture to come through, even when a standardized template is required. For example, instructors may be able to add their positionality and teaching philosophy, how they are available to students, the assignment choices students have, and transparent grading policies.

As instructors determine how best to communicate the course design via the syllabus, one important consideration will be the grading policy. A student's final grade should ultimately communicate the extent to which that student achieved the course learning outcomes. The numerical value of the assignment needs to be proportional to the scope and nature of the assignment. Thus, formative assessments—those that take place during the learning process—typically do not count much toward the final grade, as the purpose of formative assessments is to help students learn. It is important not to penalize students for not developing the necessary skills upon entry into or early in the course. Therefore, if a student does not perform well on a first lab report or quiz, the instructor will want to find ways for that student to receive feedback that does not have a significant negative impact on their final grade. On the other hand, summative assessments, which are typically required at the end of the semester and are designed to measure what was learned, could be more heavily weighted. Instructors would likely want assignments that are linked to the most important learning outcomes, or several outcomes to be more heavily weighted than less important assignments or assignments that measure only one learning outcome.

In addition to determining how much to count assignments in the final grade calculation, instructors need to determine grading policies, such as penalties for missed or late work. Instructors who aim to be culturally affirming are encouraged to be flexible with deadlines as students have complex lives. When Pasadena City College initiated a flexible late work policy, retention rates increased, especially among the Latine population (Bombardieri, 2019). If students are not permitted to submit late work, or if significant points are deducted, students may disengage or even withdraw from the course. In some cases, it may not be mathematically possible for students to pass the course when they receive no credit for an assignment. Instructors' attitudes toward late work policies can vary widely, but having flexible late or missing work policies can ensure that the final grade represents what students have learned. Many students have numerous competing responsibilities and priorities, and having some built-in flexibility can be very helpful for them. Flexible grading policies are an excellent way to be culturally affirming.

Conclusion

The brief historical context highlights why instructors need to commit to creating culturally affirming and meaningful assignments. A good first step is for instructors to consider their positionality and teaching philosophies, exploring how their perspectives and lived experiences influence their teaching actions, including the types of assignments required. Assignments are a part of the instructional design process. It takes time and effort to create assignments that honor and value students' varied cultural backgrounds and experiences, but these efforts will pay off as students will likely be more engaged and successful. Instructors are encouraged to use campus supports, such as instructional designers and teaching and learning centers, and to consult colleagues as they work on designing or redesigning their assignments. Thereafter, they will want to communicate their new course design, including assignments, in the syllabus.

Reflection Questions

1 How does the brief history synopsis presented in this chapter impact your perspective of higher education, our institutions, and your role?
2 Consider your identities and their intersections. How do they impact your positionality as an instructor?
3 What resources, such as instructional designers, are available to assist you with using backward design?
4 How well do your current learning outcomes communicate, in measurable terms, what you hope students will be able to know, think, or

do by the end of the semester? How do you communicate the link between assignments and learning outcomes to your students?
5   How do you communicate the course design through the syllabus in student-friendly ways?
6   Based on your grading system and policies, how likely is it that a student's final grade will represent the extent to which they achieved the course learning outcomes?

References

American Indian Higher Education Consortium and Institute for Higher Education Policy (1999). Tribal colleges: An introduction. https://digitalcommons.unomaha.edu/slcetribalnations/4.

Association for Supervision and Curriculum Development (2012). *Understanding by Design framework*. https://files.ascd.org/staticfiles/ascd/pdf/siteASCD/publications/UbD_WhitePaper0312.pdf.

Bombardieri, M. (2019, September 25). How to fix education's racial inequities, one tweak at a time. *Politico*. https://www.politico.com/agenda/story/2019/09/25/higher-educations-racial-inequities-000978/.

Brown, A. H., & Green, T. D. (2020). *The essentials of instructional design: Connecting fundamental principles with process and practice* (4th ed.). Routledge.

Fink, L. D. (2013). *Creating significant learning experiences: An integrated approach to designing college courses*. Jossey-Bass.

Geilman, D. J. (2018). Experiences of instructors using ready-to-teach, fixed-content online courses. Doctoral dissertation. https://digitalcommons.usu.edu/etd/7052.

Giles, M. S. (2006). Howard Thurman: The making of a Morehouse man, 1919–1923. *Educational Foundations*, 20, 105–122. https://files.eric.ed.gov/fulltext/EJ751763.pdf.

Harmon, D. A. (2012). Culturally responsive teaching through a historical lens: Will history repeat itself? *Interdisciplinary Journal of Teaching and Learning*, 2 (1), 12–22.

Harrington, C. (2022, January 25). Reflect on your positionality to ensure student success. *Inside Higher Education*. https://www.insidehighered.com/advice/2022/01/26/successful-instructors-understand-their-own-biases-and-beliefs-opinion.

Harrington, C., & Thomas, M. (2018). *Designing a motivational syllabus: Creating a learning path for student engagement*. Routledge.

Henning, G. W., & Roberts, D. (2016). *Student affairs assessment: Theory to practice*. Routledge.

Hispanic Association of Colleges and Universities (n.d.). Hispanic Serving Institutions: Definition. https://www.hacu.net/hacu/HSI_Definition1.asp.

Howe, J. (producer, writer, cinematographer) (2016, February 16). *Unspoken: America's Native American boarding schools*. Television broadcast. Utah: Public Broadcasting Service of Utah.

Johnson, A. M. (2020, October). The history of predominantly Black institutions: A primer. *CMSI Research Brief*. https://cmsi.gse.rutgers.edu/sites/default/files/History%20of%20PBIs.pdf.

Kezar, A. (2002). Reconstructing static images of leadership: An application of positionality theory. *Journal of Leadership Studies*, 8(3), 94–109.

Levin-Morales, A. (1998). *Medicine stories: History, culture and the politics of integrity*. South End Press.

Mehta, R., & Zhu, R. (2009). Blue or red? Exploring the effect of color on cognitive task performances. *Science*, 323(5918), 1226–1229.

Michael, N. A., and Libarkin, J. C. (2016). Understanding by design: Mentored implementation of backward design methodology at the university level. *Bioscene*, 42(2), 44–52.

Morales, C. R. (2021). Faculty and student success in online courses delivery: Assembling an online support team. *Papers of the 5th Canadian Conference on Advances in Education, Teaching & Technology*, 15–20. https://imrjournal.info/wp-content/uploads/2021/08/Proceedings-EduTeach2021.pdf.

Morales Irizarry, C. R. (2006). La importancia del diseñador instruccional en el diseño de cursos en línea. *Revista Didáctica, Innovación y Multimedia*, 3. https://www.raco.cat/index.php/DIM/article/view/56105.

Orlich, D. C., Harder, R. J., Callahan, R. C., Trevisan, M. S., Brown, A. H., & Miller, D. E. (2016). *Teaching strategies: A guide to effective instruction* (11th ed.). Cengage Learning.

Reigeluth, C. M., Myers, R. D., & Lee, D. (2016). The learner-centered paradigm of education. In C. M. Reigeluth, B. J. Beatty, & R. D. Myers (Eds.), *Instructional-Design Theories and Models* (Vol. 2, pp. 5–32). Routledge.

Reynolds, H. L., & Kearns, K. D. (2017). A planning tool for incorporating backward design, active learning, and authentic assessment in the college classroom. *College Teaching*, 65(1), 17–27.

Riback, C. (2021a, July 15). The 180 Podcast: Zaretta Hammond: What is culturally-responsive teaching? *PodBean*. https://turnaroundusa.org/the-180-podcast-zaretta-hammond-what-is-culturally-responsive-teaching/.

Riback, C. (2021b, August 3). The 180 Podcast: Zaretta Hammond: How teachers can become personal trainers for cognitive development. *PodBean*. https://turnaroundusa.org/the-180-podcast-zaretta-hammond-what-is-culturally-responsive-teaching/.

Sensoy, O., & DiAngelo, R. (2017). *Is everyone really equal? An introduction to key concepts in social justice education* (2nd ed.). Teachers College Press.

Sims, R. C., & Koszalka, T. (2008). Competencies for the new-age instructional designer. In J. M. Spector, M. D. Merrill, J. Merrienboer, & M. P. Driscoll (Eds.), *Handbook of research on educational communications and technology* (3rd ed.) (pp. 569–575). Lawrence Erlbaum Associates.

Swan, K., Matthews, D., Bogle, L., Boles, E., & Day, S. (2012). Linking online course design and implementation to learning outcomes: A design experiment. *Internet and Higher Education*, 81–88. doi:10.1016/j.iheduc.2011.07.002.

Thelin, J. R. (2019). *A history of American higher education* (3rd ed.). Johns Hopkins University Press.

Vavrus, M. (2008). Culturally responsive teaching. In T. L. Good (Ed.), *21st Century education: A reference handbook* (Vol. 2, pp. 49–57). Sage Publishing.

Wiggins, G., & McTighe, J. (2005). *Understanding by design* (expanded 2nd ed.). Pearson.

Woodley, X., Hernandez, C., Parra, J., & Negash, B. (2017). Celebrating difference: Best practices in culturally responsive teaching online. *Tech Trends*, 61, 470–478.

Chapter 2

What Makes Assignments Culturally Affirmative?

Adrian D. Martin

Professor Johnson stood at the front of the classroom and looked at his undergraduate students. It was his first year as a college faculty member and he was enthusiastic and excited to teach his students about American history in his U.S. History 101 course. Professor Johnson had spent hours preparing his lecture and PowerPoint slides for this class session. He hoped the students would develop an interest in (and perhaps even a passion for) American history and maybe even decide on history as a major. As a faculty member in a metropolitan area, Professor Johnson's students reflected the cultural and socioeconomic diversity of U.S. society. As he commenced this class session, and as the semester progressed, Professor Johnson continued to invest in the development of the course assignments. Yet, as the semester neared conclusion, he observed that many students demonstrated a lack of interest in these assignments. Professor Johnson realized that, despite his efforts, he needed to change his instructional planning and approach to course assignments. While he strove to demonstrate an enthusiasm for American history, he did not demonstrate a similar enthusiasm in getting to know his students as individuals, including their life experiences and cultural backgrounds. Professor Johnson began to contemplate ways to more fully integrate knowledge of who his students were into his course assignments. He recognized the need for a way to conceptualize course assignments as more than learning products, but also as opportunities to affirm his students' cultural identities.

As in the narrative above, many instructors have grappled with how to make the scope of classroom endeavors meaningful and relevant to all students. Since the 1990s, education researchers, theorists, and curriculum developers have advanced instructional frameworks that are attentive to the academic needs of culturally diverse students (e.g., Gay, 2018; Ladson-Billings, 1995; Paris & Alim, 2017; Villegas & Lucas, 2002). These frameworks provide a conceptual, epistemological, and pedagogical foundation for educators teaching students who possess a variety of life experiences and linguistic and cultural assets that differ from those of mainstream U.S. students. Whether termed "culturally

DOI: 10.4324/9781003443797-3

relevant pedagogy" (Ladson-Billings, 2014), "culturally responsive teaching" (Vavrus, 2008), "culturally sustainable pedagogy" (Alim et al., 2020), or "culturally responsible pedagogy" (Chou, 2007), these frameworks call on educators to position cultural diversity as value-laden (Banks, 2018), to provide instruction that meaningfully connects with students' identities as sociocultural and sociolinguistic individuals (Nieto & Bode, 2018), and to value multiculturalism and cultural competences as integral aspects of U.S. society (May & Sleeter, 2010).

Increasingly, attention is being given to the experiences of diverse students in higher education (Quaye et al., 2019), their sense of imposter syndrome (i.e., an inability to believe that they deserve their success or a feeling of academic fraudulence) and the institution's role in its perpetuation (Breeze et al., 2022), and how colleges and universities provide (or fail to provide) equitable learning opportunities and experiences (Patton, 2016). Indeed, frameworks for cultural responsiveness do more than support students' engagement and mastery of academic content; they advance the knowledge, skills, and dispositions requisite for *all* members of the classroom community to be able to work and learn from one another in meaningful, equitable ways (Lawrence-Brown & Sapon-Shevin, 2014). As such, culture is not limited to ethnic, national, or racial identities; instead, it encompasses a wide range of identities individuals possess (e.g., gender identity, sexual orientation, social class, neuro-diverse, diverse-ability, heritage language background, religious affiliation, regional or national identity), the ways these identities intersect (Crenshaw, 1991; Runyan, 2018), and the social communities to which students belong. Thus, these frameworks are advantageous for all learners. They provide an opportunity for all students to understand themselves and recognize cultural differences as a valuable aspect of the classroom community and, by extension, of the world outside the classroom (Martin & Spencer, 2020).

Much of the scholarly literature has attended to the underrepresentation of faculty of color (Griffin, 2019), racial and ethnic disparities in higher education attainment (Ingram & Wallace, 2019), and the decreased rates of degree completion among students of color in comparison to their White peers (Excelencia in Education, 2022; Sanchez & Kolodner, 2021). Certainly, myriad factors contribute to the current status quo, and multiple policy initiatives, institutional reforms, and pedagogical innovations are needed to address the educational inequities students of color and those from financially underprivileged backgrounds confront in higher education. Of note is that while the literature provides some insights into employing frameworks for culturally responsive teaching in higher education (e.g., Johnson, 2022; Larke, 2013), little attention has been given to how course assignments contribute to the affirmation of students' cultural identities.

This chapter explores higher education assignments conceptually as culturally affirmative learning experiences. To do so, I drew inspiration from the work of past and present scholars (e.g., Freire, 1974; Ladson-Billings & Tate, 1995; Nieto & Bode, 2018; Paris & Alim, 2017) who have endeavored to articulate the knowledge, skills, and dispositions necessary to promote equity, inclusion, and cultural responsiveness. I built upon this work and have developed principles that undergird culturally affirmative assignments. Throughout the chapter, I posit how upholding cultural affirmation connects with an assignment's learning objective. The chapter provides higher education instructors with a conceptual lens to develop equitable assignments that support students' engagement with course content and opportunities to interact productively with other members of the classroom. Culturally affirming assignments offer an avenue through which students can meaningfully employ cultural insights and understandings to advance learning and achieve academic success. Given the all too prevalent disconnect between coursework and the cultural experiences of students of color, and the limited opportunities many White higher education students have to meaningfully take up diverse cultural perspectives (Banks & Dohy, 2019), the adoption of culturally affirming assignments is long overdue.

Culturally affirming assignments are learning tasks, endeavors, and exercises that reflect a value for students' cultural identities, acknowledge how content and learning processes are culturally constructed, and uphold cultural diversity as a productive, meaningful, and generative learning asset. Culturally affirmative assignments support the learner's immediate engagement with course content and the acquisition of disciplinary knowledge and skills. Certainly, all students are cultural beings who participate in particular cultural communities. Culturally affirmative assignments are developed, enacted, and informed by an understanding of students as cultural beings and the imperative to honor their cultural capital and the cultural funds of knowledge they possess (Yosso, 2005). How these are affirmed, sustained, and leveraged through an assignment influences and affects a student's academic success. I have identified five principles for creating culturally affirming assignments (see Table 2.1).

Principle 1: Value Students' Cultural Identities

Culturally affirming assignments value students' cultural identities and positionalities (i.e., the ways in which an individual is socially situated mitigates their access to social goods or privileges) and how they employ these as learners in the classroom community. Who students are, the ways in which they identify, and how they are socially positioned should productively and meaningfully inform, shape, and affect engagement with an assignment's content, underscoring the imperative for instructors to

Table 2.1 Guiding Principles for Culturally Affirmative Assignments

Principle	Definition
Principle 1: Value Students' Cultural Identities	Who students are, the ways that they identify, and the ways in which they are socially positioned productively and meaningfully inform, shape, and affect engagement with the assignment.
Principle 2: Acknowledge the Ways Culture Informs Content and Learning Processes	Acknowledge the ways that cultural norms shape how students take up the assignment's topic or discipline, enact particular skills, or engage with the format itself. There is transparency as to how the assignment upholds (or counters) culturally dominant perspectives or orientations.
Principle 3: Uphold Multiculturalism as a Learning Asset	Recognize that engagement with multiple cultural lenses is advantageous. Students are provided insight into how others engage with, interpret, and communicate the content and skills to which the assignment attends from diverse perspectives.
Principle 4: Support Relational Engagement with Students	Meaningful engagement with course content and learning activities surfaces through purposeful and humanizing interactions between and among the instructor and students. Knowledge of who students are as individuals, as members of the classroom community, and as sociocultural beings informs the assignment.
Principle 5: Offer Diverse Ways for Students to Demonstrate Their Learning	Students are given a choice in the opportunities they have to showcase what was learned. Providing choice in the learning output maximizes students' abilities to demonstrate their understanding successfully.

know who their students are (see Chapter 4). Culturally affirming assignments proactively consider the cultural identities of students as valued assets. The assignment itself does not reflect cultural neutrality, nor does it ignore or fail to attend to who is going to work through the learning tasks. For example, a literature course might include an assignment that calls for students to explore various genres (e.g., poetry, drama, narratives). A culturally neutral assignment would expect students to engage with specific authors or literary works irrespective of who the students are. Potentially, such authors or works may reflect the dominant literary canon (i.e., the writings of male European/American authors) and ignore global literary contributions. Culturally affirming assignments would not only support students in engaging with the dominant literary canon but also provide opportunities to explore and engage with genres and authors from their own cultural backgrounds. Wendy Ostroff, for example, asks students to explore the ideas of diverse philosophers and consider how their work is interpreted by people from different backgrounds (see

Appendix, Example 10). As such, throughout the planning and development process, instructors identify, acknowledge, and value who their students are as a productive fount for learning. The assignment's structure recognizes the pedagogical value inherent in making connections with an individual's cultural identity. Students' cultural identities are a key element in the planning, development, and completion of the assignment's requirements as well as how instructors provide feedback.

The leveraging of students' cultural identities as a valued pedagogical resource reflects a sociocultural orientation to teaching and learning (Villegas & Lucas, 2002). Fundamentally, culturally affirmative assignments value who students are, their life experiences, cultural insights, and funds of knowledge as shaping and agentic elements in the learning process. Valuing these identities is reflected in how students can draw upon and make connections with their cultural selves as part of the assignment, and build upon their understanding of self in alignment with the learning objectives. For example, an assignment might call on students to assess an educational policy's impact on U.S. student achievement. Students could begin to explore the policy through an intersectional lens, considering how others from different racial, ethnic, and socioeconomic backgrounds are affected. In conjunction with this, students can be asked to frame the policy and its effects through the lens of their own schooling experiences in relation to their positionalities. In this way, affirming who students are connects with the assignment's content while also building their cross-cultural knowledge. This contrasts with a culturally neutral version of such an assignment, which would ignore the differential implications of school policies in relation to social class, race, gender, and ability. Fathia Richardson and Kathleen Polimeni ask students to explore nursing though various cultural perspectives (see Appendix, Example 9).

Valuing students' cultural identities can contribute to the likelihood of successfully satisfying the assignment's learning objectives. This does not suggest that every assignment is going to focus on students' cultural identities in and of themselves as the primary objective. It does suggest, though, that instructors should consider how, and in what ways, the content and the learning tasks in the assignment connect with who their students are as individuals and their communities. Culturally affirming assignments promote an equity-oriented dispositional orientation and enable students to bring their whole selves to the task at hand. This value is not only culturally affirming but culturally celebratory.

Valuing who students are as cultural individuals also contributes to the sustainability of their cultural communities, the cultural bodies of knowledge they possess, and the diverse ways of knowing that inform how students engage with assignments in meaningful and authentic ways (see Chapter 3). When instructors provide students with culturally affirmative assignments, the classroom environment is centered not only on the aims of the course and course content but also on the sociocultural repertoires the students possess. Throughout the planning, implementation, and evaluation processes, instructors must remain cognizant of how the assignment can incorporate, reflect, and build upon students' cultural identities and strengths. Valuing students' cultural identities can be evidenced through tasks, questions, or activities that provide opportunities for students to draw upon their own and each other's cultural repertoires (see Chapter 6).

Principle 2: Acknowledge the Ways Culture Informs Content and Learning Processes

Course content and pedagogical approaches and activities instructors employ are not acultural but rather culturally bound and situated (Gergen, 2003; Jha, 2012; Stigler & Hiebert, 1999). The ways in which teachers interact with their students, in which students interact with each other, and in which academic content is presented, discussed, and applied are all connected with particular cultural values, norms, and perspectives, usually those of the dominant culture (Banks, 2018). It is paramount that instructors are cognizant of and consider how culture and tacit cultural assumptions guide and inform the assignments students are expected to complete. Instructors need to acknowledge how, and in what ways, particular cultural norms shape how students take up the topic or discipline and enact particular skills, or even the format that is employed for an assignment (see Chapter 5). This suggests not only that the assignment is responsive to the cultural identities and communicative norms of students, but also that the assignment (in terms of both content and what it calls for students to do) is transparent as to how it upholds (or counters) culturally dominant perspectives or orientations (see Chapter 7).

Culturally affirmative assignments acknowledge how content reflects specific cultural perspectives or norms. For example, a history lesson might take up the topic of Christopher Columbus and other European explorers' journeys to the Americas. A culturally affirmative assignment would showcase how the presentation of this topic reflects assumptions. In this example, the use of the term "New World" invokes a European perspective, as the Americas would not constitute a new world for the indigenous population. Uncritical employment of the term "New World" therefore reinforces a European cultural perspective and its corollary assumptions. This reflects a need for instructors to appraise how language is used. Culturally affirmative assignments call for a critical examination of how an assignment's content and format are accessible (or inaccessible) to students, and if these are related to cultural differences. Students gain the opportunity to critically appraise, question, problematize, and theorize alternative means of disciplinary content representation. Diana Recouvreur challenges students to consider the racial and cultural implications of how quantitative data is used (see Appendix, Example 18).

It is important for instructors to proactively consider the funds of knowledge students possess. In other words, instructors must avoid making assumptions about what students know (or do not know) concerning the assignment, and students' abilities to engage with the content or the tasks involved. To support students' success, instructors need to provide direct and timely guidance (see Chapter 8) with appropriate scaffolds in culturally meaningful ways.

Culturally meaningful scaffolds can assist students' ability to complete an assignment. For example, a mathematics instructor may provide students with an assignment that calls on them to solve a series of equations. The syntax or mathematical notation that is employed in North America is not universal. In this example, many students are of cultural backgrounds that do not employ the North American notational system. The assignment could require students to solve the equations using multiple notational systems—those they are familiar with from their heritage culture and those used in the United States. Subsequent feedback offered to the students is also provided in ways that are accessible (see Chapter 8). For some, written feedback might be appropriate; for others, individual conferences with the instructor might be more useful. In these ways, how content is culturally structured is made explicit and students are provided with opportunities to explore this while working toward the assignment's objectives.

This principle emphasizes the importance of articulating how content is constructed or presented and demonstrating transparency (through direct instruction or instructional materials or resources) as to how the assignment reifies (or fails to reify) particular cultural norms. Potentially, instructors can provide students with opportunities to explore this aspect of the assignment's content. Showcasing, discussing, analyzing, or elaborating on how the presentation of content is culturally bound is a starting point for considering other diverse cultural constructions (see Chapters 5 and 7).

Principle 3: Uphold Multiculturalism as a Learning Asset

Upholding multiculturalism as a learning asset is a powerful and equity-oriented lens that strengthens the ability to interpret content and how particular skill sets are enacted, valued, and utilized among a variety of social groups in different regional or geographic settings. Whereas Principle 1 emphasizes the cultural identities of students who are completing the assignment, this principle emphasizes cultural diversity at large. Thus, it extends beyond the identities of students and instructors in a classroom. Culturally affirming assignments uphold multiculturalism by recognizing that engagement with multiple cultural lenses is advantageous to members of the classroom community. As such, multiculturalism is value-laden and enriches the learning opportunities of all students. Assignments that uphold a multicultural orientation are pedagogically efficacious in supporting students' work toward satisfying, meaningful understanding and achieving the assignment's learning objectives. Furthermore, upholding multiculturalism promotes inclusive and affirmative social and communal engagement (Lawrence-Brown & Sapon-Shevin, 2014), which is integral for the enactment of democratic practices in a diverse society (Strom & Martin, 2022). Just as culturally affirmative assignments reflect a value for who students are, and the cultural insights and orientations they possess, they also utilize the affordances of multicultural perspectives as a learning tool. They provide students with insights into how others engage with, interpret, and communicate the content and skills that the assignment attends to from diverse perspectives. Students are thus able to engage in perspective-taking. For example, Theresa Haug-Belvin encourages students to reflect not only on the intersectionality of their own identities but also on how these impact leadership actions (see Appendix, Example 16).

Another example is a class assignment in an urban planning course that requires students to assess the work of Robert Moses, a chief constructor for many of New York City's major twentieth-century public projects. Normatively, such an assignment would require students to assess the overall impact of these public works (e.g., highways, tunnels) upon the city. However, incorporating multiculturalism might call on students to assess the impact and effect of these projects from the perspective of the people and communities where they were built. In this example, this would include African American, Hispanic, and working-class White communities. It could also spotlight how individuals with physical disabilities were impacted. Such an assignment could extend this analysis into the present and consider which social groups (including social classes) have benefited the most from these projects, and which have been disenfranchised. Students could also research how advocates or leaders among these different communities have responded to, appraised, or critiqued these public projects. This type of assignment offers opportunities for students to engage with multicultural perspectives and enriches their understanding of the content.

This principle allows students to rethink and consciously take stock of their cultural stance (as well as those of others), understanding, and appreciation of the assignment's content. Perspective-taking has long been highlighted as a productive instructional approach that supports students' ability to engage in deep thinking (Wolgast et al., 2020). Subsequently, students can translate this skill into other contexts.

Upholding multiculturalism as a learning asset promotes an instructional and educational experience that can foster cross-cultural competencies. Given the increasingly diverse U.S. population and the persistent issues of racial discrimination and socioeconomic disparities correlated with race, it is paramount that all students build cross-cultural competencies. Culturally affirmative assignments can help to support students' capacity to interact, work, and live with others who are different from themselves. This can enable dispositions among members of the classroom community that are inclusive, inviting, and celebrate cultural diversity as an opportunity to grow and learn. Students gain greater insight into themselves and others throughout the learning process and draw from the well of their cultural funds of knowledge to make meaningful connections with diverse individuals and communities (see Chapter 3).

Principle 4: Support Relational Engagement with Students

I concur with hooks (1994), McLaren (2015), and Noddings (2013) that meaningful engagement with course content and learning activities surfaces through purposeful and humanizing interactions between and among instructors and students. Such interactions are consistent and ongoing, beginning before students engage with assignments and extending after assignment completion (see Chapter 4), at which point an instructor would review the submission, provide feedback, and issue a grade. It is important to emphasize that this process occurs among individuals and is ultimately relational, highlighting the fact that the assignment's efficacy to promote student learning is contingent upon the nature of the interactions and interconnectedness between an instructor and their students (Harrington, 2021). Cognizance of relational engagement suggests instructors must know who their students are as individuals, as members of the classroom community, and as sociocultural beings. Relational engagement forefronts the importance of an instructor reflecting upon who they are, demonstrating respect and empathy, enabling students to grow and learn, and maintaining an openness to learn alongside their students (Kitchen, 2005). Scott Mattingly and Nadia Bhuiyan describe how they use a life-story assignment to learn about and connect with their students (see Appendix, Example 5).

Promoting relational engagement means instructors consider and take into account who their students are, and how the assignment calls for students to communicate, take up, and relate information, or demonstrate a skill set. Reflecting on relational engagement calls attention to whether students will work collaboratively with each other, work with the instructor, or work independently. A culturally affirmative assignment allows forms of engagement that make space for students to utilize their cultural assets (i.e., the cultural knowledge, skills, and insights they possess; see Chapter 4). Relational engagement suggests instructors plan for how content will be presented, and how students are expected to interact and engage with an assignment.

Relational engagement enables students to participate actively in the learning endeavor and to grow as learners. Insight into students' cultural selves informs the assignment's design, how students are expected to interact with and take up the instructional tasks, and how the assignment is evaluated. The essential learning goals, the cultural identities students possess, and how students can be honored through their interactions with the assignment, their peers, and the instructor should all be considered as part of the learning process. This calls attention to the need to consider the interactive and communication modes that students use to investigate, analyze, or highlight how content is culturally constructed. Instructors should assess how students are expected to engage with disciplinary content and skills as culturally bound, and if students have the necessary support to do so via the ways in which they are expected to work with the content and/or each other. In other words, students are provided with opportunities to learn about the nature of the discipline as culturally bound and can engage with the assignment, with their peers, and with the instructor in meaningful and productive ways.

For example, consider an instructor who is teaching a course on public speaking. An assignment calls for students to give a speech where the aim is to convince the audience of a particular perspective. The students in this class are linguistically diverse, with many speaking English as a second (or third) language. The instructor reflects upon their own experiences speaking in front of groups and how, given that they are a native speaker of English, the task of speaking publicly in English is far more accessible to them than it is to many of the students in the class. Drawing on this understanding, the instructor elects to provide the students with choices on the assignment and opportunities to practice their speeches in pairs, small groups, and even in their heritage languages before presenting the speeches to the whole class. The instructor demonstrates a relational sensitivity to who the students are and provides pathways for assignment completion to support and promote their learning.

This ethic of demonstrating respect and interacting with one's students through relational engagement positions reflection as key to developing and implementing culturally affirmative assignments. Instructors must reflect upon their own identities and positionalities, and how their knowledge and understanding of students and themselves as sociocultural individuals informs participation and learning (Harrington, 2022; see also Chapter 1). Reflecting on positionality can help instructors understand their professional roles and responsibilities, the purpose of the assignment, and potential tensions or difficulties that might surface with the assignment. Specifically, instructors should be cognizant of the socioemotional responses that content might elicit among students. While this might be more readily apparent with assignments centered on controversial topics or issues of social injustice, it is relevant in all areas of study, given that students bring their cultural identities to all assignments.

Principle 5: Offer Diverse Ways for Students to Demonstrate Their Learning

The fifth principle for culturally affirming assignments holds that students are provided with diverse ways to demonstrate their learning. The demonstration of learning is the learning output—what students are expected to create, do, or demonstrate to showcase their knowledge or skills. This can surface in multiple ways beyond traditional exams, such as in presentations, podcasts, and infographics (see Chapter 5). Demonstrations of learning should provide students with choice in the opportunities they have to showcase what was learned; providing choice in demonstrations of learning helps maximize students' abilities to demonstrate their understanding successfully (see Chapter 6). Instructors can draw on their insights of who their students are, and the cultural strengths and assets they possess, and utilize these as productive resources to showcase what was learned. Considering diverse ways of demonstrating learning builds bridges between the cultural identities of students in relation to the content or topic under study. In conjunction with this, instructors can provide feedback that is meaningful and supportive (see Chapter 8). As such, feedback calls attention not only to areas in need of improvement but also to areas of strength. Furthermore, feedback should provide recommendations for continued learning and growth. This hearkens to the work of others who have theorized frameworks on cultural responsiveness (Gay, 2018; Villegas & Lucas, 2002) and reinforces the ethic of knowing and valuing who the students are (see Chapter 4).

Another means of supporting this principle is to give students opportunities to reflect, comment on, or illustrate how the presentation of content and skills are culturally bound in their demonstration of learning. This could be included as an element that informs how students engaged with the assignment and the steps or instructions throughout the process of working on it. For example, a biology course might include an assignment where students are expected to demonstrate their understanding of the four stages of mitosis. This demonstration of learning can be accomplished in multiple ways, such as a report, a presentation, poetry, hip-hop, or a digital slideshow. Students can choose what format to employ to demonstrate what they learned. In this way, students showcase their knowledge of mitosis in a format or mode that is meaningful and engaging to them. As such, students can develop proficiency and expertise not only in the privileged and dominant disciplinary norms but also through norms that align with diverse cultural orientations.

Conclusion

The five guiding principles for creating assignments that are culturally affirming are as follows: valuing learners' cultural identities; acknowledging how culture informs content and learning processes; upholding multiculturalism as a learning asset; supporting relational engagement; and offering diverse ways for students to demonstrate their learning. I have described how these principles can be enacted and promoted. Instructors who are committed to providing a culturally supportive, responsive, and sustainable learning environment can consider how they can develop assignments that reflect and support cultural affirmation. Certainly, the manifestation of these principles will surface in different ways depending on an assignment's learning objective, discipline, and students' academic needs.

The value, importance, and learning opportunities inherent in culturally affirming assignments are of benefit to all members of a classroom community. Students benefit from participating in a learning endeavor that is responsive to diverse cultural identities and the cultural strengths individuals possess. Culturally affirming assignments can help students develop a deeper understanding of what they are learning while simultaneously making connections between themselves, others, and course content.

It is hoped that instructors will take up, adopt, and utilize the principles offered in this chapter to guide and inform their assignments. Certainly, this is of value not only pedagogically but also in the pursuit of educational equity. The more fully course content and assignments can meaningfully intersect with an individual's cultural identity and offer opportunities to consider the intersections of culture with course content and with others, the more likely it will be that the learning experience resonates with the learner and contributes to their engagement as an informed citizen in our multicultural democracy. Other researchers and scholars should explore, expand upon, and further investigate the lens provided. By more fully implementing and utilizing culturally affirmative assignments, the value of the learning task extends beyond the scope of the immediate context; it fosters the validation of self and others and cultural plurality as hallmarks of the learning experience and social engagement. I believe that culturally affirmative assignments are one important means by which instructors can promote equitable learning experiences for their students. I hope that the principles discussed in this chapter can be employed by instructors in service to their students and in service of a better world.

Reflection Questions

1   How do your course assignments currently reflect the principles for culturally affirmative assignments?

2   How can you more fully utilize your knowledge about who your students are to develop or revise culturally affirmative assignments?
3   In what ways do your values for education, teaching, and learning connect with the principles for culturally affirmative assignments?
4   How can you collaborate with colleagues and students to explore course assignments and how these are or could be culturally affirmative?
5   What questions do you have about your professional practice and course assignments in relation to cultural affirmation? What action steps can you take to address your questions?

References

Alim, H. S., Paris, D., & Wong, C. (2020). Culturally sustaining pedagogy: A critical framework for centering communities. In N. Nasir, C. Lee, R. Pea, & M. McKinney de Royston (Eds.), *Handbook of the cultural foundations of learning* (pp. 261–276). Routledge.

Banks, J. A. (2018). *An introduction to multicultural education* (6th ed.). Pearson.

Banks, T., & Dohy, J. (2019). Mitigating barriers to persistence: A review of efforts to improve retention and graduation rates for students of color in higher education. *Higher Education Studies*, 9(1), 118–131. https://doi.org/10.5539/hes.v9n1p118.

Breeze, M., Addison, M., & Taylor, Y. (2022). Situating imposter syndrome in higher education. In M. Breeze, M. Addison, & Y. Taylor (Eds.), *The Palgrave handbook of imposter syndrome* (pp. 1–16). Palgrave.

Chou, H. (2007). Multicultural teacher education: Toward a culturally responsible pedagogy. *Essays in Education*, 21(1), 139–162. https://openriver.winona.edu/eie/vol21/iss1/13/?utm_source=openriver.winona.edu%2Feie%2Fvol21%2Fiss1%2F13&utm_medium=PDF&utm_campaign=PDFCoverPages https://openriver.winona.edu/cgi/viewcontent.cgi?article=1213&context=eie.

Crenshaw, K. (1991). Demarginalizing the intersection of race and sex: A Black feminist critique of antidiscrimination doctrine, feminist theory and antiracist politics. *University of Chicago Legal Forum*, 1(8), 139–167. http://chicagounbound.uchicago.edu/uclf/vol1989/iss1/8.

Excelencia in Education (2022). Latino college completion: United States. https://www.edexcelencia.org/research/latino-college-completion.

Freire, P. (1974). *Education for critical consciousness*. Continuum.

Gay, G. (2018). *Culturally responsive teaching: Theory, research, and practice* (3rd ed.). Teachers College Press.

Gergen, K. J. (2003). Knowledge as socially constructed. In M. Gergen & K. J. Gergen (Eds.), *Social construction: A reader* (pp. 15–17). Sage.

Griffin, K. A. (2019). *Race and ethnicity in higher education: A status report*. American Council in Education. https://ace.e-wd.org/resources/ideas-and-insights/redoubling-our-efforts-how-institutions-can-affect-faculty-diversity/.

Harrington, C. (2021). *Keeping us engaged: Student perspectives (and research-based strategies) on what works and why*. Routledge.

Harrington, C. (2022). Reflect on your positionality to ensure student success. *Inside Higher Education*. https://www.insidehighered.com/advice/2022/01/26/successful-instructors-understand-their-own-biases-and-beliefs-opinion

hooks, b. (1994). *Teaching to transgress: Education as the practice of freedom*. Routledge.

Ingram, L., & Wallace, B. (2019). "It creates fear and divides us": Minority college students' experiences of stress from racism, coping responses and recommendations for colleges. *Journal of Health Disparities Research & Practice*, 12(1), 80–112. https://digitalscholarship.unlv.edu/jhdrp/vol12/iss1/6.

Jha, A. K. (2012). Epistemological and pedagogical concerns of constructionism: Relating to the educational practices. *Creative Education*, 3(2), 171–178. http://dx.doi.org/10.4236/ce.2012.32027.

Johnson, A. P. (2022). Culturally responsive teaching in higher education. *International Journal of Equity and Social Justice in Higher Education*, 1, 25–29. https://doi.org/10.56816/2771-1803.1008.

Kitchen, J. (2005). Conveying respect and empathy: Becoming a relational teacher educator. *Studying Teacher Education*, 1(2), 197–207. https://doi.org/10.1080/17425960500288337.

Ladson-Billings, G. (1995). Toward a theory of culturally relevant pedagogy. *American Educational Research Journal*, 32(3), 465–491. https://doi.org/10.3102/00028312032003465.

Ladson-Billings, G. (2014). Culturally relevant pedagogy 2.0: A.k.a. the remix. *Harvard Educational Review*, 84(1), 74–84. https://doi.org/10.17763/haer.84.1.p2rj131485484751.

Ladson-Billings, G., & Tate, W., IV (1995). Toward a critical race theory of education. *Teachers College Record*, 97(1), 47–68. https://eric.ed.gov/?id=EJ519126.

Larke, P. (2013). Culturally responsive teaching in higher education: What professors need to know. *Counterpoints*, 391, 38–50. http://www.jstor.org/stable/42981435.

Lawrence-Brown, D., & Sapon-Shevin, M. (Eds.) (2014). *Condition critical: Key principles for equitable and inclusive education*. Teachers College.

McLaren, P. (2015). *Life in schools: An introduction to critical pedagogy in the foundations of education* (6th ed.). Paradigm Books.

Martin, A. D., & Spencer, T. (2020). Children's literature, culturally responsive teaching, and teacher identity: An action research inquiry in teacher education. *Action in Teacher Education*, 42(4), 387–404. https://doi.org/10.1080/01626620.2019.1710728.

May, S., & Sleeter, C. E. (Eds.) (2010). *Critical multiculturalism: Theory and praxis*. Routledge.

Nieto, S., & Bode, P. (2018). *Affirming diversity: The sociopolitical context of multicultural education* (7th ed.). Pearson.

Noddings, N. (2013). *Caring: A feminine approach to ethics and moral education*. University of California Press.

Paris, D., & Alim, H. S. (Eds.) (2017). *Culturally sustaining pedagogies: Teaching and learning for justice in a changing world*. Teachers College Press.

Patton, L. D. (2016). Disrupting postsecondary prose: Toward a critical race theory of higher education. *Urban Education*, 15(3), 315–342. https://doi.org/10.1177/0042085915602542.

Quaye, S. J., Harper, S. R., & Pendakur, S. L. (Eds.) (2019). *Student engagement in higher education: Theoretical perspectives and practical approaches for diverse populations* (3rd ed.). Routledge.

Runyan, A. S. (2018). What is intersectionality and why is it important? *Gender on Campus*, 104(6), 10–14. https://www.jstor.org/stable/26606288.

Sanchez, O., & Kolodner, M. (2021). Why White students are 250% more likely to graduate than Black students at public universities. *Hechinger Report*. https://hechingerreport.org/%E2%80%8B%E2%80%8Bwhy-white-students-are-250-more-likely-to-graduate-than-black-students-at-public-universities/.

Stigler, J., & Hiebert, J. (1999) *The teaching gap: Best ideas from the world's teachers for improving education in the classroom*. The Free Press.

Strom, K. J., & Martin, A. D. (2022). Toward a critical posthuman understanding of teacher development and practice: A multi-case study of beginning teachers. *Teaching and Teacher Education*, 114, 1–11. https://authors.elsevier.com/sd/article/S0742051X22000592.

Vavrus, M. (2008). Culturally responsive teaching. In T. L. Good (Ed.), *21st-century education: A reference handbook* (Vol. 2, pp. 49–57). Sage Publishing.

Villegas, A. M., & Lucas, T. (2002). *Educating culturally responsive teachers: A coherent approach*. State University of New York Press.

Wolgast, A., Tandler, N., Harrison, L., & Umlauft, S. (2020). Adults' dispositional and situational perspective-taking: A systematic review. *Educational Psychology Review*, 32(2), 353–389. https://doi.org/10.1007/s10648-019-09507-y.

Yosso, T. J. (2005). Whose culture has capital? A critical race theory discussion of community cultural wealth. *Race, Ethnicity, & Education*, 8(1), 69–91. https://doi.org/10.1080/1361332052000341006.

Chapter 3

What Makes Assignments Meaningful?

Bridget Arend and Erika R. Carlson

Marta, a college sophomore, sits down to work on the class assignment for a history course. She frequently tunes out in class because there seems to be no connection between this course and anything she feels she needs to be learning right now. She admits to feeling resentful for having to take this required core course, which just seems to take her more into debt and further away from a job in the growing healthcare field. She keeps trying to focus her attention on the assignment, which asks her to summarize the causes of a historical conflict. But after a lot of time without any progress, and needing to get to her part-time job, she finally turns to the Internet and new generative artificial intelligence tools that can produce a summary paper in minutes.

How can instructors create college assignments that are meaningful to their students? First, what does meaningful mean? The word can have many definitions, most of which suggest that when something is meaningful it has a purpose or useful quality, or that it is in some way important or significant. In this chapter, we describe various ways that course assignments can be meaningful through the exploration of five principles for creating such assignments. We developed these principles based on the expansive literature about how humans learn and effective teaching practices for college-level learning. The principles are rooted in adult learning theory, psychology, cognitive science, neuroscience, the Scholarship of Teaching and Learning, and theories about culturally responsive pedagogy. Assignments can be most effective when they are perceived to be useful, have a purpose, contribute to the important goals of higher education, and are significant to students' lives and lived experiences.

It is useful to consider the principles of adult learning when creating meaningful assignments. According to the National Student Clearinghouse Research Center (2022), the average age of undergraduate students in the United States is 24 and the average age of graduate students is 32. Since the 1950s, many scholars, most notably Malcolm Knowles, have attempted to bring together learning from the social sciences, psychology, and adult education to develop best practices for teaching these adult

DOI: 10.4324/9781003443797-4

learners. Andragogy has been defined as the art and science of helping adults learn, in contrast to pedagogy, which has been considered the art and science of teaching children (Knowles, 1980). According to andragogy theories, adults resist being passive recipients of learning and instead thrive in self-directed and relevant learning environments that involve problem-centered, experience-based, and immediate application of their learning to their lives and careers. Adults learn effectively when they can be self-directed in settings that value their experiences (Knowles et al., 2005).

A strong principle of andragogy is the idea of immediate relevance. Adult learners have a life-centered orientation and are more motivated when they believe their learning will be immediately applicable. They want to learn practical skills that will help them solve real-life problems. Similarly, they are more motivated when they can personally identify with what they are learning and believe the learning is valuable. Andragogical principles recognize that adults have a strong need to know why they are learning something. Although learners of all ages can be intrinsically motivated to engage in learning for learning's sake, when engaged in formal learning experiences, adult college students value learning that helps advance life goals, whether personal or professional (Knowles et al., 2005).

These universally accepted principles have been expanded by Kenyon and Hase (2001), who argue that andragogy is limited by the fact that it does not incorporate self-determined learning—heutagogy. A heutagogical approach means that the learner drives what they need to know in a rapidly changing society; their learning goes beyond the classroom and is transferable to the work environment (Kenyon & Hase, 2001). This self-determined learning approach emphasizes flexibility in learning and challenges the learner to design and negotiate the learning plan.

These guiding ideas of andragogy and heutagogy align with what has been learned about learning from cognitive science and developmental psychology studies, which have indicated that learning is most effective when it is relevant, engaging, and interactive (Ambrose et al., 2010). Effective learning happens in learning-centered environments where students make connections to authentic, real-world tasks (National Research Council, 2000). Students intuitively know this. In a recent large study about student engagement, over half of the undergraduate students surveyed admitted that they were struggling to remain engaged in their classes (Hines, 2023). The students shared that they were seeking learning experiences that were current, relevant, and applicable to the real world. In other words, they wanted assignments that had a purpose and that they believed were useful.

In addition, meaningful assignments have the potential to be significant in terms of how students view their society, environment, and the world around them (see Chapter 2). As Fink (2013, p. 34) explained, if we think of learning as creating some sort of change in the learner, significant learning "requires there be some kind of lasting change that is important in terms of the learner's life." Mezirow (1997) theorized that adults have acquired a body of experiences, which include the concepts, values, feelings, and frames of reference that define their habits of mind and how they see the world. Children can be taught to see relationships, think abstractly, and become critically aware, but it is often not until adulthood that learning involves awareness of one's assumptions and frames of reference with the intent of critically reflecting upon and changing one's worldviews. This type of transformative learning has the potential to be life-changing, and thus truly meaningful.

Meaningful assignments can challenge students to think critically, possibly even change their worldviews, and can build important skills for their careers. Unfortunately, though, college assignments are not universally viewed as meaningful. Melzer's (2014) study of over 2,000 writing assignments from 400 courses at 100 different institutions found that more than 80 percent had a purpose that was considered "transactional," with the teacher as the only intended audience. When students do not see assignments as useful, purposeful, or important, they may lack the motivation to take those assignments seriously. The most memorable college learning experiences are not the rote quizzes or formulaic papers that are all too often experienced in college but rather those activities and projects that are perceived as useful due to their current and future-focused, real-world relevance. These are the assignments that result in important, significant learning (see Chapter 5).

Guiding Principles for Meaningful Assignments

Based on theories and studies from adult learning and the learning sciences, we have developed five guiding principles to help faculty design meaningful college assignments (see Table 3.1).

Principle 1: Aligned with Learning Outcomes

Colleges and universities work diligently to create a comprehensive curriculum with carefully constructed program-level learning outcomes. This process requires the creation of curriculum maps and strategic pathways so that each course a student takes has learning outcomes that support the program goals. Course learning outcomes need to feed into program learning outcomes so that graduates walk away with the desired knowledge, skills, and abilities.

The backward course design process developed by Wiggins and McTighe (2005) is frequently used. In this process, instructors begin by determining what they desire for their students to think, know, or do by

Table 3.1 Guiding Principles for Meaningful Assignments

Principle	Definition
Principle 1: Aligned with learning outcomes	Meaningful assignments help students see the connections between their assignments and course-level and program-level learning outcomes. They align not only with the content students need but also with the skills and contexts within which students will use their knowledge and skills.
Principle 2: Personally relevant and culturally affirming	Meaningful assignments allow students to make connections between what they are learning and their personal and professional lives. They value students' diverse backgrounds, lived experiences, and prior knowledge, and allow students to tap into their interests when demonstrating learning.
Principle 3: Challenging, empowering, and growth-focused	Meaningful assignments present the "just right" level of challenge for students. They allow students choice to foster autonomy and increase motivation, and help students develop a positive growth mindset toward their learning.
Principle 4: Authentic with real-world value	Meaningful assignments are situated within real-life contexts and are designed to represent authentic situations. They are forward-looking by showing what students can do with their knowledge and skills in the future.
Principle 5: Skill-based and relevant to the world of work	Meaningful assignments help students develop in-demand career skills that are relevant to their interests. They align with the skills that students will need in their future careers.

the end of each course. These course outcomes need to align with the broader program and institutional goals. After careful consideration of the overall course goals, instructors next think about how they will know if students have achieved these goals. In other words, they ask themselves: "What evidence do I need to see?" This step results in identifying the course assignments, often referred to as assessments, and includes the activities that students "turn in" for grades or complete to receive formative feedback. Finally, the course activities are created, providing students with the practice they need to be able to do well on the course assignments.

Assignments within a course are opportunities for students to demonstrate their achievement of or progress toward the course learning outcomes (see Chapter 1). Collectively, across the curriculum, assignments serve as measures of success toward the overall program and institutional goals. When aligned to the outcomes of a course or program, they serve as direct, measurable indicators of learning.

Instructors will want to explicitly communicate the connections between assignments and both course and program learning outcomes to students. Seeing connections between their current learning tasks and the ultimate goals of the course and program can increase student motivation. Instructors are encouraged to map assignments to course outcomes to validate alignment. See Table 3.2 for an example of how a psychology assignment is linked to course learning outcomes. Instructors can communicate these connections in various ways, such as sharing the map on the syllabus or adding a sentence or two about how the assignment will help students achieve the course and program learning outcomes in the assignment description.

Clear purpose statements for each assignment are also recommended (see Chapter 7). Purpose statements provide the *why*—or rationale—for the assignment. Explicitly sharing what students will learn and be able to do as a result of an assignment, along with why this knowledge or skill set holds future value, is an excellent way to engage and motivate students.

Meaningful assignments should not only align with content goals—*what* is to be learned—but also match the desired type of learning—the *how* of learning. For example, although assignments such as quizzes or recall tests best support knowledge acquisition goals, such tests would likely not be the most meaningful way for students to demonstrate complex problem-solving skills or professional judgment. Instead, case studies

Table 3.2 Example of Assignment and Course Learning Outcomes Alignment Map for Psychology Research Course

Assignment Description	Analyze the ethical issues raised in psychology research using the principles of the APA	Critically evaluate published empirical research studies	Evaluate the advantages and disadvantages of experimental designs and other research approaches used in psychology
Critically analyze the ethical implications of Milgram's Obedience Study research design	I	R	—
Develop a research proposal that includes experimental design and procedure	—	M	R

Note: I = Introduced; R = Reinforced; M = Mastered.

and projects might be better indicators of whether students can analyze a situation and draw upon theory and research to determine the best course of action (Davis & Arend, 2012). Reflective essays, for example, can show critical thinking, whereas journals can demonstrate changes in values. Different types of assignments are needed for different types of course learning outcomes.

In addition to having alignment, it is important that the outcomes themselves are meaningful and fulfilled in a way that is both useful and significant. For example, students often immediately see the value of assignments that help them develop technical skills. When an accounting major is asked to do accounting problems, this type of assignment will likely be perceived by the student as meaningful. But in some cases, the technical skills emphasized in assignments do not match the skills needed by college graduates. For example, only approximately 10 percent of students who graduate with a psychology major earn a doctorate degree in psychology, yet the curriculum is designed for this small segment of the population. A typical program or course outcome for psychology majors at most colleges or universities is to develop statistical reasoning skills, and students taking psychology courses will often have assignments requiring them to run statistical analyses using SPSS software, yet this may be an outcome that most psychology graduates do not need. It may be more meaningful to help students develop statistical reasoning skills using Excel software, as competency with this program is desired by many business employers, and many psychology graduates find careers in the business field.

Similarly, meaningful assignments should not ignore learning outcomes' more difficult-to-assess aspects. Learning outcomes such as applying research principles to be an informed consumer in the real world, developing the principles of an ethical practitioner, or active involvement with diverse communities support the essential college learning outcomes defined by the Association of American Colleges and Universities (AAC&U). Assignments that support these outcomes create those truly memorable and transformative experiences for students. They also provide opportunities for faculty to create meaningful connections between theoretical constructs and tangible post-course applications. Truly rich learning experiences are those that support multiple goals in a reinforcing way (Fink, 2013). Adding a few personal reflection questions to an assignment can support ethical decision-making. A case study analysis that teaches technical skills may also help students explore ethical reasoning, and make personal connections to the content.

Principle 2: Personally Relevant and Culturally Affirming

In addition to connecting to significant course and program outcomes, meaningful assignments are personally relevant and culturally affirming.

Adult learning principles assume that learners draw on personally relevant life experiences to assist in learning new information and are more motivated when their experiences are valued (Knowles, 1980). Martin (Chapter 2) suggests that culturally affirming assignments value learners' cultural identities, acknowledge how culture informs content and learning processes, uphold multiculturalism as a learning asset, support relational engagement, and offer diverse ways for students to demonstrate their learning. Students need assignments that make personal connections, affirm their lived experiences, value multiple forms of prior knowledge and experience, and are asset-based.

Assignments can be personally relevant when students see how what they are learning connects to their personal and professional lives. In the Meaningful Writing Project, a multi-year investigation into what made writing meaningful for students, the participants noted that assignments were meaningful when the subject matter was personally interesting and they were able to make connections between what was being learned and their interests and lives beyond school (Eodice et al., 2017). They further described assignments that helped them engage with content deeply and tapped into their own experiences or histories as engaging. Data from this project also indicated that social and relational relevance was important, meaning the students perceived their learning to be relevant to their friends, family, and/or communities (Eodice et al., 2019). Additional examples come from Judy C. K. Chan, who uses an exploring favorite foods assignment to help students learn the course content in a way that is personally and culturally meaningful (see Appendix, Example 7), and Meredith May, who asks students to explore local history through individual stories and then contribute their historical knowledge in the archives of a local museum (see Appendix, Example 11). Eodice et al. (2019, p. 1) noted that meaningful writing assignments can "capitalize on the experiences, beliefs, and aspirations students bring to their learning."

Students may not immediately see the connections between an assignment and their lives, so it can be very helpful for instructors to convey the numerous potential benefits of the assignment and find ways for students to discover the application and relevance for themselves. To help students see the meaning of assignments, instructors can share examples of how the knowledge and skill learned through the assignment can have personal, cultural, and professional relevance. Instructors may also want to share what other students have found valuable about the assignment and encourage students to reflect on the potential value of the assignment in their personal and professional lives.

When making these personal connections, instructors strive to make their assignments relevant to students, yet what has value and feels relevant to instructors may not always be what motivates students. Often instructors' backgrounds and identities are not the same as those of their students, who enter classrooms with myriad identities, past experiences, and aspirations. It is important to recognize and honor these varied lived experiences and professional goals when developing assignments. For example, knowing students' prior knowledge is important when designing learning and assignments (Ambrose et al., 2010). The concepts of funds of knowledge and cultural wealth described by Martin (Chapter 2) provide useful frameworks for understanding the different types of knowledge and strengths that students bring to their classrooms. Similarly, knowing students' varied backgrounds and future interests can help instructors adjust assignments so that they take a form that is well suited to their students' different life paths (see Chapter 4). George and Thompson (Chapter 6) argue that assignment choice makes it easier for students to explore aspects of the content that are relevant to their own cultures or interests.

Meaningful assignments not only help students learn content and skills but can also increase their sense of belonging (Strayhorn, 2018). Students feel more belonging in a learning environment when their assignments validate their experiences. Students who see that assignments are personally relevant and culturally affirming will be more likely to exert higher levels of effort and, as a result, will be more likely to achieve the course learning outcomes.

Students appreciate personalized assignments. In a creative approach with a large class, Pietryka and Glazier (2022) used projects where students themselves gathered data on relevant and timely topics, such as reactions to political advertisements or social network connections. The instructor then shared the aggregate data with the class, as well as personalized reports created through an automated program so students could see how their findings compared with those of their classmates. Students reported both learning more from this assignment and enjoying it more than other assignments.

Principle 3: Challenging, Empowering, and Growth Focused

Meaningful assignments challenge students and push their thinking and abilities in ways that are empowering and achievable. Ideally, assignments are not too difficult and not too easy. Vygotsky's zone of proximal development is a useful concept that describes the space between what a learner can do without assistance and what a learner can do with guidance or other types of support (Vygotsky & Cole, 1978). Students can feel lost when the assignment task is too advanced for their current learning state and they are not provided with adequate support, or, alternatively, can feel bored when assignments are not challenging enough. Assignments should aim for the "just right" level of challenge for students.

Meaningful assignments that are within the student's zone of proximal development need to be accompanied by scaffolded support to help students experience success (see Chapter 8). One way to support students is through transparency. As Wasserman and Ayeni (Chapter 7) point out, transparency is an equity-minded approach that requires instructors to articulate the purpose, tasks, and criteria of assignments. These assignment details can provide students with a clear roadmap of what is expected and how to get there (Felten & Finley, 2019). Transparency reduces the cognitive load of an assignment while also providing an equitable chance to achieve the learning goal.

In addition to being appropriately challenging, meaningful assignments are empowering. One effective way to empower learners is through choice. Students have emphasized that being allowed to choose what type of academic product to complete increases their ownership and investment in the assignment (Harrington, 2021). According to adult learning theory, adults need to be involved in the planning and evaluation of their instruction. In the Meaningful Writing Project, having the autonomy to decide what to write about or how to write about something increased student motivation and engagement (Eodice et al., 2017). Similarly, the principles of Universal Design for Learning (UDL) suggest that providing students with choices in how they engage with and represent their learning supports diverse learners (Morin, 2018).

Assignments can empower students to take actions that they would not have taken otherwise. For example, students have noted that they would not have participated in events if they were not required to do so during an assignment (Harrington, 2021). Assignments can stretch students to go outside their comfort zones and develop new skills. For example, requiring students in a first-year seminar to conduct informational interviews with professionals in the field is a way to help students develop or expand their network and develop essential networking skills while learning about career options. Students may not feel comfortable asking others about their careers, but asking others to help them with an assignment might be an easier task. Similarly, having students present their research findings from an experiment they conducted in a sociology class provides learners with an opportunity to answer critical questions from classmates about their research process and may give them the confidence they need to submit their work to a conference.

A key goal of adult education is to develop autonomous, responsible thinkers (Mezirow, 1997). Students need to be able to adapt to different life and work situations. Experts rely on metacognition—or awareness of one's own thinking processes—to continually learn and grow. Not all students arrive in college with the same level of learning strategies or metacognition skills, so a typical classroom is unlikely to have "metacognitive equity" (McGuire, 2021). However, such thinking skills can be taught, and assignments can be used to help students develop them. For example, Caralyn Zehnder used a reflections and connections assignment in a biology course to develop these skills (see Appendix, Example 6). Another way to support students' development of metacognitive skills is to require them to self-assess their work using a provided rubric (see Chapter 8). Assignments that help students become aware of, monitor, and adjust their learning processes are meaningful and can create agency and autonomy in the learner.

Meaningful assignments focus on the process of learning and amplifying a growth mindset for learners. A growth mindset helps students understand that success in college takes effort, and when students believe that their abilities can grow and develop over time, they will perform better (Dweck, 2006). As the concept of mindsets has evolved in recent years, it is becoming even more clear that students' beliefs and effort need to be combined with trying out new learning strategies and getting input on their effectiveness (Dweck, 2015). The construct of a growth mindset is anchored in one's belief that one can do better and typically affirmed by others. Nevertheless, prominent scholar Luke Wood has pointed out that many underserved learning populations do not receive ongoing affirmations of their intelligence, so the notion of nurturing a growth mindset through assignments should be navigated through this lens (Hilton, 2017). It is important for instructors to recognize that effort alone may not lead to success as many students, especially students of color, face systemic racism barriers that influence educational outcomes.

In the same spirit of ongoing growth and learning, meaningful assignments should also foster the development of long-lasting learning as opposed to surface-level learning that disappears when the semester ends. Studies comparing experts and novices show differences mainly in how knowledge is organized (National Research Council, 2000). Novices may have sparse, superficial, and disconnected knowledge structures, whereas experts have rich, meaningful, and integrated knowledge structures. How knowledge is organized may be more important than knowing in the first place. Assignments that simply help students collect a pile of knowledge will be less meaningful than those that help students make connections and build sophisticated knowledge structures that they can use in the future. Lunden E. MacDonald required students to create concept maps to connect key points from the lecture and reading before participating in an online discussion on fascism in Spain (see Appendix, Example 14).

Principle 4: Authentic with Real-World Value

Meaningful assignments authentically build relevance and real-world context. Fink (2013) used the term "forward thinking" to describe authentic tasks. In contrast to traditional forms of assessment that look back on what was learned, essentially aiming to ensure that students learned what was covered, forward-looking assessments ask students to look ahead to what they will be able to do in the future as a result of learning. When using forward-looking assignments, the instructor imagines how students will use the skills and knowledge in their careers and uses assignments to provide those practice opportunities. According to Wiggins (1998), an assignment is authentic if it is realistic, requires judgment and innovation, asks the student to "do" the subject, simulates as much as possible the context in which the student will use the skills in the workplace or civic or personal life, assesses the student's ability to utilize knowledge and skills to negotiate a complex task, and provides opportunities to rehearse, practice, consult resources, get feedback, and refine their product or performance. Authentic assessments are not only more interesting to students but more valid in terms of what students will do with their new knowledge and skills both now and in the future.

Hanstedt (2018) stressed that assignments are meaningful if they require students to make meaning, integrate and synthesize, make decisions or take action, and, most importantly, do all of this in the context of uncertainty. He emphasized that students need to be prepared for a world with complex problems, and that this requires complexity in the classroom. Authentic assignments, by their nature, provide that complexity.

Adults are more motivated to learn when they see an immediate benefit from engaging in a learning task. The benefits of some assignments are obvious, such as when a computer science programming lesson teaches students to write code and this new skill can be immediately applied in their current work situation. Articulating the real-world value of assignments becomes more important when the benefits are less obvious, or the application of knowledge and skills is not immediate. Instructors may share why learning is necessary or how it could be useful in the future, connect classroom learning to the world of work, or add reflective questions to an assignment to help students make such connections themselves. Giving students a taste of how they will use their newfound skills in the future should help them see the real-world value of assignments.

Creating more relevant and authentic assignments can also be achieved by extending the audience beyond just the instructor. Too often, assignments are seen only by the instructor. Requiring assignments to be viewed by other faculty, industry stakeholders, or publicly via social media can add relevance and real-world context. For example, Kayla, an undergraduate student, noted that her instructor required students to create a sexual education curriculum that would be used by the community (Harrington, 2021). The assignment was submitted not only to the instructor but also to the director of a community organization, and Kayla stated that knowing it would benefit members of the community motivated her.

Students may be asked to share their work with an industry partner, at a conference event, or even simply with peers in the classroom. Just imagining they are developing a proposal for a committee, speaking to a group of students, or writing to a public official makes the assignment more meaningful and adds real-world complexity. Shalini Srinivasan asked students to share what they learned about a topic of their choice in a formal letter to an elected official, even though they were not required to send the letter (see Appendix, Example 8). Similarly, Marie-Therese C. Sulit and Charles Zola increased meaning by having students present their poster assignment at a campus-wide event (see Appendix, Example 15).

Principle 5: Skill-Based and Relevant to the World of Work

Employers focus on skills, yet, in higher education, the focus is on outcomes. Skill development is often infused into outcomes, but skills are rarely the primary focus. Meaningful assignments are designed to help students develop essential skills they will need professionally. Harrington and Thomas (2018) encouraged instructors to list the skills that will be developed for each assignment on the syllabus. This explicit communication can help students see the value of the assignment and develop skill-based language that will be useful when interviewing for positions. When students have options for how to share their products, different skills may be identified. For example, a course learning outcome might state that students will be able to summarize research on stress reduction techniques. If students are allowed to present their findings through a formal presentation, the related skills might include finding and evaluating information, synthesizing findings, developing visually effective slides, presenting the information orally, and using audience engagement strategies. If the assignment option was to create a website, many of the same skills would be developed, but instead of presenting the information orally and using audience engagement skills, skills relating to webpage creation would be developed.

Unfortunately, there is often a misalignment between job opportunities and college graduates' skill sets (Flaherty, 2021). To bridge this gap, public–private partnerships such as the one between New York Jobs CEO Council and CUNY have been created. In this type of partnership, employers and faculty backward map curriculum to real-time, in-demand skills so students are career ready and more competitive candidates for early career positions with family-sustaining wages. Providing students with assignments that will demonstrate tangible skills that are robust and desired by talent acquisition teams across industries allows adult learners to amplify their voice and communicate their transferrable skills confidently when they pursue employment.

Faculty will be better able to create assignments that focus on essential career skills if they know their students and their career aspirations (see Chapter 4). Working within the bounds of their department and what is in their control, instructors can explore the most common technical and professional skills that undergird the varying fields within their discipline. One approach to learning about the skills that are needed in the field is collaborative, with students asked to engage in a job search and analyze the skill requirements on recruitment postings. This type of activity can help students learn about the positions that are currently available in the field and the skills they need to be highly qualified candidates. As the students seek out different types of positions based on their career aspirations, faculty will learn more about their students while also staying abreast of industry requirements. Students could also be asked to identify the top skills noted in the job descriptions and then explore how they will develop these skills through the various course assignments. Meanwhile, faculty could make tangible efforts to incorporate skills that are currently missing from assignments.

Assignments can be used to help students develop transferable essential and career skills. Examples of transferable essential skills include problem-solving, analytical reasoning, critical thinking, leadership, adaptability, communication, teamwork, creativity, project management, active listening, and writing. A career—or technical—skill is specific to a particular field or industry. Examples for a data scientist would be knowledge of multiple programming languages and coding skills required for working in relational databases. An example of a transferable essential skill for this data scientist would be succinct, unambiguous, and concise writing that enables them to share their findings clearly. Both transferable essential and career skills are needed.

There is considerable evidence that employers are seeking employees with transferable essential skills. For example, in a survey conducted for the AAC&U, nearly all employers (91 percent) agreed that, for career success, "a candidate's demonstrated capacity to think critically, communicate clearly, and solve complex problems is more important than his or her undergraduate major" (Hart Research Associates, 2015, p. 6). Even more employers (96 percent) insisted that "all college students should have experiences that teach them how to solve problems with people whose views are different from their own" (Hart Research Associates, 2015, p. 4).

Instructors who want to ensure that they are creating assignments that will help students develop career-focused skills will likely find it helpful to review national competencies that articulate the various skills sought by employers. For example, the National Association of Colleges and Employers (NACE) competencies, which were co-created by a task force of college career services staff and industry recruiting professionals, focus on what it means to be career ready after college graduation. Ultimately, the task force recommended eight core competencies (see Table 3.3).

Instructors can leverage the NACE competencies by identifying one or more competencies that align with a course learning outcome for an assignment. Once identified, the assignment could be reviewed through

Table 3.3 National Association of Colleges and Employers (NACE) Competencies

Competency	Definition	Behavioral Example
Career and Self Development	One's awareness of strengths and weaknesses and ability to cultivate professional relationships internal and external to an organization.	Professionally advocate for oneself and others. Intellectual curiosity and eagerness to learn.
Communication	Ability to share ideas succinctly and information effectively with both internal and external stakeholders.	Employ active listening, persuasion, and influencing skills.
Critical Thinking	Identify and respond to needs based on a fundamental understanding of context and a comprehensive analysis of relevant information.	Make decisions and solve problems using sound, inclusive reasoning and judgment. Ability to adapt and prioritize in a rapidly changing environment.
Equity and Inclusion	Demonstrate awareness, skills, and knowledge to create an inclusionary environment and equitably engage with others.	Ability to be open and inclusive of diverse ideas and thinking.
Leadership	Maximize individual and others' strengths to achieve goals.	Encourage, influence, and motivate self and others under a common goal.
Professionalism	Recognize cultural and social norms of the work environment and act in an interest that positively affects the workplace.	Lead with integrity and accountability to self, others, and the organization. Demonstrate dedication and dependability to stakeholders and the organization.
Teamwork	Develop and maintain relationships to work effectively toward shared goals.	Demonstrate active listening, collaboration, and accountability.
Technology	Navigate and leverage technologies to increase effectiveness.	Willingness to learn and incorporate new technologies for a streamlined approach to goals.

Source: Adapted from National Association of Colleges and Employers (2023)

the lens of making that skill development more explicit to students. Additionally, each NACE competency has a corresponding assessment rubric that both students and instructors can use for progress evaluation of developing each behavior. Students can self-assess at the start to better understand where they may need to grow to reach a level of mastery for each competency. Instructors can create assignments that explicitly allow for growth across these competencies and ultimately create deeper meaning for students through completion.

Instructors who are in a position to review and update learning outcomes are encouraged to revise course and program outcomes to ensure they incorporate a combination of transferable essential and career skills and meet the needs of industry partners. Although many instructors, especially part-time instructors, must work with established learning outcomes, there is often some latitude in the pedagogical approach to assignments. In such cases, instructors can think about how to give students the option to demonstrate their learning in ways that will facilitate the development of these career skills.

Conclusion

Returning to the example that opened this chapter, Marta was unable to see a connection between her history assignment and her future career. Most history instructors likely feel passionate about the need for students to learn history and the great relevance of historical events to their current situations, contexts, future careers, and lives as productive citizens. These goals should ideally form part of the course learning outcomes and can then be supported within assignments that align with these goals of relevance and future skill development. Perhaps the instructor could have assigned a presentation that connected the causes of this historical conflict with a modern-day conflict or a cultural example chosen by the students. The instructor could also have incorporated discussions or reflections that helped Marta see how the skills of synthesis and analysis will be useful in her future healthcare career. If Marta had been given an assignment that provided relevance, appropriate skill development, and choice, she may have taken personal ownership of it.

Meaningful assignments not only align with learning outcomes but are personally relevant and culturally affirming. They are challenging, empowering, and growth-focused, authentic with real-world value, and focus on skills that are relevant to the world of work. They are practically useful, memorable, and significant. It may not be possible for every assignment to include all the principles of meaningful assignments outlined in this chapter, but every instructor should strive to provide students with assignments that have a relevant purpose, develop useful career skills, contribute to the important goals of higher education, and are significant to their future lives.

Reflection Questions

1 How can you help students see the connection between your assignments and course-level and program-level learning outcomes?
2 In what ways do your assignments allow students to make connections between what they are learning and their personal and professional lives?

3 How can you show that you value students' prior knowledge and lived experiences with assignments?
4 How do you determine the "just right" challenge level for assignments?
5 How can you help students develop a growth mindset through assignments?
6 In what ways are your assignments authentic and forward-looking?
7 To what extent are your assignments situated in a real-world context?
8 How do your assignments help students develop in-demand career skills?
9 What NACE competencies will students develop through your assignments?

References

Ambrose, S. A., Bridges, M. W., DiPietro, M., Lovett, M. C., & Norman, M. K. (2010). *How learning works: Seven research-based principles for smart teaching*. John Wiley & Sons.

Davis, J. R., & Arend, B. D. (2012). *Facilitating seven ways of learning: A resource for more purposeful, effective, and enjoyable college teaching*. Routledge.

Dweck, C. S. (2006). *Mindset: The new psychology of success*. Random House.

Dweck, C. (2015). Carol Dweck revisits the growth mindset. *Education Week, 35*(5), 20–24.

Eodice, M., Geller, A. E., & Lerner, N. (2017). *The meaningful writing project: Learning, teaching and writing in higher education*. University Press of Colorado.

Eodice, M., Geller, A. E., & Lerner, N. (2019). The power of personal connection for undergraduate student writers. *Research in the Teaching of English, 53*(4), 320–329.

Felten, P., & Finley, A. (2019). *Transparent design in higher education teaching and leadership: A guide to implementing the transparency framework institution-wide to improve learning and retention*. Routledge.

Fink, L. D. (2013). *Creating significant learning experiences: An integrated approach to designing college courses*. John Wiley & Sons.

Flaherty, C. (2021, April 5). What employers want. *Inside Higher Ed*. https://www.insidehighered.com/news/2021/04/06/aacu-survey-finds-employers-want-candidates-liberal-arts-skills-cite-preparedness.

Hanstedt, P. (2018). *Creating wicked students: Designing courses for a complex world*. Routledge.

Harrington, C. (2021). *Keeping us engaged: Student perspectives (and research-based strategies) on what works and why*. Routledge.

Harrington, C., & Thomas, M. (2018). *Designing a motivational syllabus: Creating a learning path for student engagement*. Routledge.

Hart Research Associates (2015). Falling short? College learning and career success. https://dgmg81phhvh63.cloudfront.net/content/user-photos/Research/PDFs/2015employerstudentsurvey.pdf.

Hilton, A. A. (2017, November 12). Prominent scholar calls growth mindset a "cancerous" idea in isolation. *Huffington Post*. https://www.huffpost.com/entry/prominent-scholar-calls-growth-mindset-a-cancerous_b_5a07f046e4b0f1dc729a6bc3.

Hines, B. (2002). The state of the student: Adjusting to the "new normal" … and all that comes with it. https://www.wiley.com/en-us/network/trending-stories/the-state-of-the-student-adjusting-to-the-new-normal-and-all-that-comes-with-it.

Kenyon, C., & Hase, S. (2001, March). Moving from andragogy to heutagogy in vocational education. https://eric.ed.gov/?id=ED456279.

Knowles, M. (1980). *The modern practice of adult education: Andragogy versus pedagogy*. Cambridge Adult Education.

Knowles, M. S., Holton, E. F., III, & Swanson, R. A. (2005). *The adult learner: The definitive classic in adult education and human resource development*. Routledge.

McGuire, S. (2021). Close the metacognitive equity gap: Teach all students how to learn. *Journal of College Academic Support Programs*, 4(1), 69–72. doi:10.36896/4.1ep1.

Melzer, D. (2014). *Assignments across the curriculum: A national study of college writing*. Utah State University Press.

Mezirow, J. (1997). Transformative learning: Theory to practice. *New Directions for Adult and Continuing Education*, 74, 5–12.

Morin, A. (2018). Universal design for learning (UDL): What you need to know. *Understood*. https://www.understood.org/en/articles/universal-design-for-learning-what-it-is-and-how-it-works.

National Association of Colleges and Employers (2023). What is career readiness? https://www.naceweb.org/career-readiness/competencies/career-readiness-defined/.

National Research Council (2000). *How people learn: Brain, mind, experience, and school* (expanded ed.). National Academies Press.

National Student Clearinghouse Research Center (2022). Current term enrollment estimates: Spring 2022. https://nscresearchcenter.org/wp-content/uploads/CTEE_Report_Spring_2022.pdf.

Pietryka, M. T., & Glazier, R. A. (2022). Learning through collaborative data projects: Engaging students and building rapport. *Education Sciences*, 12(12), 897. http://dx.doi.org/10.3390/educsci12120897.

Strayhorn, T. L. (2018). *College students' sense of belonging: A key to educational success for all students*. Routledge.

Vygotsky, L. S., & Cole, M. (1978). *Mind in society: Development of higher psychological processes*. Harvard University Press.

Wiggins, G. (1998). Ensuring authentic performance. In G. Wiggins, *Educative assessment: Designing assessments to inform and improve student performance* (pp. 21–42). Jossey-Bass.

Wiggins, G., & McTighe, J. (2005). *Understanding by design* (expanded 2nd ed.). Pearson.

Chapter 4

Getting to Know Your Students
A First Step in Creating Culturally Affirming and Meaningful Assignments

Shantell Strickland-Davis and Jairo McMican

Makena and Lucas sat nervously outside an office waiting for their instructor to arrive. The instructor had asked both to come by for ten minutes to discuss their first assignment. The instructor showed up and asked "the happy one" to come in first. Makena and Lucas looked at each other with confused expressions. The instructor then gestured at Makena and said, "You mentioned your family was from Kenya in the getting-to-know-you activity and I looked up the meaning of your name." The smile stretched across Makena's face from ear to ear. Most of her past educators had never even bothered to say her name correctly, let alone remember it or learn its meaning. Makena had been questioning whether attending college was the right decision for her and this affirmed that she had chosen well.

As Lucas sat there waiting for Makena to finish with the instructor, his anxiousness and curiosity grew. He was also considering dropping out and concentrating on working. As Makena left the office, smiling, she wished Lucas and the instructor farewell. Lucas entered the room, and his eyes were immediately drawn to a picture on the wall from a television show he had liked growing up. The instructor noticed this, and they had a conversation about their mutual admiration for the show. Then they got to the heart of the meeting. The instructor wanted to express their appreciation for Lucas's effort on the assignment. They used the same terminology that Lucas had employed in the "what I value" activity. Lucas mentioned that his grandmother's approval meant a lot to him, so the instructor suggested that she would likely be proud of the work and sacrifice he was making. The instructor continued that college will be difficult at times, but well worth it. Right then and there, Lucas decided to do whatever it took to graduate.

This chapter will focus on the importance of instructors getting to know their students and some of the ways in which they may do so. It is difficult, if not impossible, to create affirming assignments if instructors do not know their students. Students are more successful academically when they feel seen and believe that they matter (Hernandez, 2021; Schlossberg, 1989). Being seen and heard are vital aspects of student belonging (Museus et al., 2017) and institutions that intentionally support their students in this

DOI: 10.4324/9781003443797-5

way have higher persistence rates. Yes, students can indeed be supported by a variety of offices at an institution. However, most higher education employees know that the greatest impact often comes from the relationships that develop through the classroom, whether that be virtual, hybrid, or in-person. The first section of this chapter focuses on these relationships and their influence on student success. Those that follow focus on impactful strategies for setting up and maintaining instructors' commitment to their students.

Role of Relationships in Learning

Researchers have consistently demonstrated the important role of instructor–student relationships in student success outcomes. For example, Bonem et al. (2020) found that the quality of instructor–student interactions was more important than the teaching methods used in terms of student satisfaction, motivation, course evaluations, and academic performance as measured by grades in courses. Further evidence comes from Demir et al. (2019), who found that instructor–student rapport predicted students' perception of the course and how much they believed they learned.

Positive messaging, authentic care, and proactive interventions produce higher rates of success because students tend to put in more effort when they feel validated and believe that their instructors care about them as people (White et al., 2015). Comments such as "You are producing powerful work" and "I am so fortunate to have you in this class" can be highly beneficial motivators for students. Such comments need to come from a place of authenticity to have value, though. Research has shown that student perception of their instructor's caring mattered more than other variables, such as grit, that have previously been connected to student success outcomes (Buskirk-Cohen & Plants, 2019).

There are many ways that instructors can get to know their students and communicate their care. Early actions before the semester begins and at the start of the semester can be especially important in developing instructor–student relationships. These relationships can then be nurtured throughout the semester and maintained after the class ends. The better instructors know their students and connect with them, the more likely it is that they will create assignments that are culturally affirming and meaningful to their students.

Strategies for Developing Instructor–Student and Student–Student Relationships

Before Class Begins

The student–instructor relationship can be established before the first day of class. Through intentional preparation, instructors can take action to promote an inclusive and culturally responsive learning environment. First, they can focus inward and use reflective practice to determine their positionality and teaching philosophy and frame their instruction. They can then find ways to learn about their students before they even meet them in class. Thereafter, they can conduct a diversity audit of their assignments and teaching practices and make revisions as needed to ensure that the learning tasks are culturally affirming and meaningful. The Culturally Affirming and Meaningful Assignments Checklist may prove useful in this process (see the Introduction). Finally, instructors can share course resources before the semester begins.

Strategy 1: Review, Reflect on, and Update Positionality and Teaching Philosophy Statements

Instructors are encouraged to reflect on their positionality and teaching philosophy and how their various identities and lived experiences are similar to or different from those of their students. Positionality refers to an instructor's varied social identities and their influence on their behavior (Taylor et al., 2000). Although most educators may think of positionality in terms of research, Harrington (2022) advocated for instructors to reflect on their positionality by reflecting on their group memberships, roles, and experiences and how these identities influence their teaching actions. Positionality reflection also involves instructors considering any potential biases they may have. Considering, acknowledging, and reflecting on biases, and especially their impact on teaching, is an important first step in creating an inclusive learning environment. By being more cognizant of biases, instructors can be more intentional in their course design and approach (Steele, 2011).

A teaching philosophy includes an instructor's personal beliefs and values about teaching (Laundon et al., 2020). Through a teaching philosophy statement, an instructor clarifies their role as a teacher, communicating their expectations and beliefs about teaching and learning, and generating excitement and enthusiasm about the learning process. A teaching philosophy serves as a vehicle for sharing teaching motivation and purpose and conveys that the instructor is committed to growth and improvement (Hegarty, 2015). It is important for instructors to update these statements before the start of each semester because they will continue to evolve as educators.

Engaging in constructive self-reflection allows instructors to better understand how their positionality and teaching philosophy impact their approach to content, their colleagues, and their students. After engaging in this reflective process, instructors can modify course documents such as the syllabus, assignments, and other materials as well as their approach to teaching so that it is more inclusive and aligned with the needs of diverse student populations. Before the start of the semester, instructors can share their positionality and teaching philosophy to help students get to know them and discover what they can expect to learn and experience in the class. These early actions can help instructors develop good relationships and rapport with their students.

Strategy 2: Learn about Your Students before You Meet Them

Getting to know your students as much as possible before the semester begins is critical. One way to start this process is by reviewing the students' demographic data on the college's website to get a general understanding of who is attending the institution. Instructors may also have access to student rosters prior to the start of the semester. Depending on the level of access to these rosters, they may be able to determine the diversity of their classes in terms of race, ethnicity, age, major or program of study, and time in school. An instructor may also consider where their course falls in terms of a student's overall academic journey. For example, it may be one of the first courses the student is taking at college, or it could be an option after the completion of several prerequisite courses.

Spending time understanding students' varied academic preparation levels can help instructors structure their classes in a way that is supportive and inclusive. Instructors can review the learning outcomes of prerequisite or co-requisite courses, and they can meet with instructors teaching those classes to learn more about the knowledge and skills the students developed while taking them. Martin (Chapter 2) emphasizes the importance of knowing the prior knowledge that students bring to the classroom. For example, instructors can determine if the students on their course have a shared foundational knowledge achieved through prerequisite courses, or if student background knowledge varies significantly.

In addition to considering what transpired before the current course, instructors will want to think about how the learning in this course will need to serve the students well in future coursework. For example, if an instructor teaches an introductory course for a particular discipline, they may consider incorporating an assignment that not only aligns with their own course outcomes but also prepares the students for success in an advanced course they will likely take in the future (see Chapter 3).

In addition to consulting institutional student demographic data, instructors might email their students to request further information about themselves. Researchers have found that reaching out to students in this way resulted in increased student motivation, more positive perceptions of faculty, and even higher levels of student persistence (Legg & Wilson, 2009). Flanigan et al. (2022) discovered that educators utilized virtual resources to establish relationships with their students, identify shared interests, and exchange knowledge to foster rapport.

Getting to know students means learning about their interests, abilities, attitudes, values, and cultural strengths (Hernandez, 2021; Yosso, 2016). Another way instructors can get to know their students before the start of the semester is by asking them to respond to a survey with questions about their interests, beliefs, values, strengths, and aspirations. Students have noted that they appreciate it when their instructors make an effort to get to know them via surveys and then use what they learn to make the learning experience more personalized (Harrington, 2021). M. Geneva Murray uses a survey assignment to help her formulate the best type of support for her students (see Appendix, Example 1).

The relationships instructors create and nurture in their classrooms support a student's sense of belonging and connection. Learning about students enables instructors to create inclusive learning environments. The more instructors know about their students, the easier it will be for them to determine what types of assignments and learning activities will be perceived as culturally affirming and meaningful by their students.

Strategy 3: Conduct a Diversity Audit of Course Materials, Including Assignments

Regularly reviewing course materials to identify any hidden forms of oppression and ensure the inclusion of diverse perspectives is critical. Muñiz (2020) reminded us that culturally responsive teachers constantly evaluate materials and resources to safeguard against the perpetuation of stereotypes and the misrepresentation or unintentional exclusion of certain identity groups. One valuable approach is to conduct a diversity audit on assignments and other course materials.

Although diversity audits are typically conducted at the institutional level (Chun & Evans, 2019), instructors can also review course documents and teaching approaches by practicing cultural humility. Diversity audits involve asking a lot of questions, such as:

- Whose voices and perspectives are represented in course readings, lectures, and assignments?
- Whose voices and perspectives are missing?
- In what ways are different cultural perspectives valued or devalued through assignments and other learning tasks?

The Culturally Affirming and Meaningful Assignments Checklist (see Introduction) can be a useful tool when conducting a diversity audit of assignments. The goal of the audit process is to encourage instructors to determine where improvements can be made. As a result of engaging in this process, instructors can modify assignments or teaching approaches to make them more inclusive for all students.

Strategy 4: Share Introductory Course Resources

In addition to engaging in self-reflective processes and modifying assignments as needed, instructors who share course resources before the start of the semester help students connect with themselves and their courses. When an instructor records an introductory video, for example, students can see the instructor's passion and enthusiasm. Introductory videos can also provide students with information about the instructor's background, areas of interest, and teaching approach. In addition, students can be introduced to the course learning outcomes and activities they should expect. Although videos are often preferred because much is conveyed via non-verbal communication, students can also learn about their instructor and the course through other means, such as blog posts and emails. Instructors can use introductory course resources to establish a welcoming tone and approachable presence (Harrington & Thomas, 2018). First-generation students and those who are unsure if they belong in college will likely find these introductory resources highly beneficial.

The hierarchical structure of a classroom automatically distances instructors from students; as a result, students may feel intimidated by their instructors. To combat this, it is important for students to get to know their instructors. In an interesting study by Gehlbach et al. (2016), students who were informed about five similarities they had with their teachers at the start of the semester were more likely to report better relationships with those teachers and performed better in the course than students who did not learn of such similarities. Indeed, the researchers reported closing equity gaps by 60 percent using this strategy (Gehlbach et al., 2016).

Instructors who take the time to humanize their relationship with students and share information about themselves set the stage for a productive instructor–student relationship and a successful semester. The more instructors share, the more likely it will be that their students will find something they have in common with them (Hernandez, 2021). For instance, if an instructor reveals that they were a first-generation scholar, students who are also first-generation may find it reassuring to have this in common with their professor. Instructors may opt to share their positionality and teaching philosophy statements during introductory videos or messages so that students can learn more about them and how their identities influence their teaching methods. It can be very motivational for students when their instructors show that they care and are committed to their students' success.

Introductory videos and related resources are most useful when they provide students with information about their instructor and the course. Introductory course resources, such as the syllabus and "getting-started" modules, can help students understand what is expected of them and how to begin. Some instructors opt to do a screencast that explains how to access course materials within the learning management system or how to access campus resources. This type of introductory resource can be very helpful to students. Screencast software can capture a small screen showing the instructor while they share their full computer screen illustrating course resources. Screencasts have been used in many ways, including introducing students to courses, illustrating concepts or resources while lecturing on course topics, and providing feedback to students (Pinder-Grover et al., 2011; Ruffini, 2012). A variety of introductory resources, including screencasts, can help students understand how to begin engaging with class materials and their peers.

When developing these introductory course resources, instructors should ensure that the language within the documents is student-friendly and inclusive. For example, it is better to use the phrase "student hours" rather than "office hours" because many first-generation students (and others) may interpret the latter as those times when educators are in their offices and do not want to be interrupted. "Student hours" more readily communicates the message that this time has been set aside for the students. Harrington and Thomas (2018) suggested personalizing the language in course documents such as the syllabus. For example, "instructor and student" could be replaced with "I and you" to personalize the document. These types of personalized resources communicate that the instructor cares about their students, which helps students develop good relationships with their instructors and discover the actions they need to take to be successful.

Early in the Semester Strategies for Getting to Know Students and Developing Relationships

Getting to know students requires educators to create a space for this to occur early on in virtual, hybrid, and in-person classes. During these initial interactions, instructors might engage in disarming—an approach that involves ensuring students know that the instructor wishes to welcome them and not cause them any anguish (Virtue et al., 2021). Although instructors can engage in disarming by making welcoming comments and alleviating potential fears or concerns, environmental factors play a role in this process, too. All of the items or artifacts in an environment have meaning, tell stories, and convey cultural norms. Instructors can culturally affirm students through the books on their shelves, the pictures, posters, signs, and other items displayed on classroom walls, and even the backgrounds in virtual meetings. Therefore, it is well worth analyzing these environments to cultivate non-verbal cues that validate students and inform them that their new instructor is delighted that they chose this course to further their academic journey.

It is important for instructors to dedicate class time at the beginning of the semester to develop a rapport and relationships with their students, and for students to develop relationships with their peers. Early actions, such as intentional "getting-to-know-you" activities on the first day, using a personalized approach to communicating with students, and meeting with students individually, will enable instructors to foster productive relationships with—and gain valuable insights into—their students. These relationships and insights can be very useful in the creation of assignments that are culturally affirming and meaningful.

Strategy 1: Dedicate Class Time to Getting-to-Know-You Activities

On day one, instructors will want to make time to get to know their students personally and academically, and for students to get to know each other. One of the first steps in creating an inclusive classroom environment is getting to know the correct pronunciation of students' names and their preferred pronouns. "People respond more positively to their name being used. It shows that they matter" (Kunjufu, 2009, p. 24). Instructors should create a space for students to share their pronouns in a way and at a time that is best for them. Asking students to share publicly "on the spot" may force those who are unsure of their preferred pronoun to make a decision that they subsequently regret, or could even result in outing a student who is not ready to share on day one (Levin, 2018).

As instructors engage with their students in the first few days and get to know them, it is important to learn about, acknowledge, and affirm the strengths they bring to the classroom. These strengths (and subsequent opportunities) are not always academically focused. Making time to learn about each student's interests and values, discover their responsibilities outside of school, and gather information about their previous learning successes helps instructors create a more meaningful learning environment.

Many different types of activities can be used on day one to learn about students and foster instructor–student and student–student connections. One example is the 4×4×4 approach, developed by Jairo McMican. This refers to four strengths, four challenges, and four values. In the first or second meeting of the course, instructors can ask their students to list four academic strengths they have demonstrated or experienced throughout their academic journey. Some examples could be coming to class on time or encouraging their classmates. Next, instructors ask their students to list four challenges or obstacles they have had to overcome in their academic journey. These can be either personal or academic in nature. For example, students might say balancing single parenting with studying, anxiety when taking tests, or working full-time while in school. Next, instructors ask their students to list four of their most important values or four of their most important reasons for taking the course or furthering their education. Again, the students can choose to share either academic or personal values. In addition to asking students to reflect on their strengths, challenges, and values during an early class, instructors could ask them to continue the conversation in an online discussion or even as an assignment. This connector activity can give the instructor insights into who is in their classroom—information that may prove useful in identifying relevant examples that can be incorporated into lessons, classroom discussions, and feedback. For example, if a student listed their family as a top value, the instructor could provide feedback such as "You really did well on this assignment. Your family must be super proud of the effort you are putting into this."

Another introductory activity that can help instructors learn about their students is the Pecha Kucha. A traditional Pecha Kucha is a fast-paced presentation of 20 slides, each of which can be shown and discussed for no more than 20 seconds (Pecha Kucha, n.d.). Harrington (2021) recommended a modified version of this for introductions, with fewer slides used so that it does not take up as much class time. If class time is a concern, students can also post their Pecha Kucha introductions in the learning management system. Instructors could model the Pecha Kucha approach by sharing information about themselves and then asking students to convey whatever personal and/or professional information they would like to share about themselves. Researchers have found that more information can be communicated in less time using this structured presentation style (Liao et al., 2020). One student, Shadiquah, noted that this activity helped her learn about her classmates in a much deeper way than traditional ice-breaker activities because many students shared information about their cultural backgrounds and values (Harrington, 2021).

In another activity—"Capturing Cultural Bias" (Pedersen, 2004)—instructors display a list of adjectives that are routinely related to various cultures, such as "aggressive," "patriotic," "obedient," "talkative," "competitive," "quiet," and so forth. Next, they ask which adjectives the students like and dislike, where and from whom they learned about them, and, finally, whether it would be possible to change their feelings about them. This activity can enhance students' awareness of what they find favorable and allow them to self-reflect on how their opinions were formed.

Having students partner with their peers to discuss answers to questions is another great way for instructors to get to know their students and for students to get to know one another. Although this technique is already widely used, it can be adapted to have a stronger cultural focus. For example, students are generally asked to share their names, majors, and interests during these introductory conversations, but they could also be encouraged to share the origins of their names, particular traditions of their cultures, how their cultures celebrate success or show support, or something that most people would not know about them merely by looking at them. After sharing their responses with a classmate or two, students can be invited to share one response with the whole class. It can be helpful to give students a list of potential questions and allow them to respond only to those they are happy to answer. Another useful strategy is to ask face-to-face students to continue their dialogue in an online discussion. For online students, the discussion forum—potentially with the use of videos in addition to written responses—works well for this activity.

Any activity that helps students connect with one another while also preparing them for the type of work they will face throughout the semester is a good use of class time. For example, if an instructor is planning to use Jigsaw Classroom group work during the semester, they can use this process during an introductory activity. Harrington and Thomas (2018) noted that a Jigsaw activity on the syllabus could be a great way to help students learn about the class, connect, and discover how this group activity works. The syllabus Jigsaw involves assigning students in home base groups to different pages or sections of the syllabus and then having them switch into expert groups with other students who were assigned to the same pages or sections. During the expert group discussion, students review their assigned section of the syllabus and determine the key points they want to share with their home base group members. When students move back to their original home base groups, each student spends a couple of minutes highlighting the most important elements of their assigned sections of the syllabus. After students complete this part of the activity, they can be encouraged to share what they are most looking forward to in the class and what they are concerned about. The key points of this discussion could be shared anonymously on an index card or using a technology tool like a Google document. Instructors can then review the students' responses and determine ways to provide clarification, support, and encouragement to alleviate any concerns raised.

Instructors can also use assignments to get to know their students early on in the semester. For example, Emily Murai asks her students to complete a "Your Story" assignment, in which each student writes about a meaningful event in their life (see Appendix, Example 2). Another example comes from Camille Locklear Goins. who gets to know her students through a personal artifact assignment that requires them to identify an artifact that communicates their leadership style and cultural values and then discuss this with their peers (see Appendix, Example 3).

Strategy 2: Use Personalized Language

It is well worth investing the necessary time to learn all the students' names by the second class. Although this can be a difficult task, especially in large classes or if the teaching load is heavy, students have reported appreciating the effort that faculty put into learning their names, noting that this personalizes their learning experience (Cooper et al., 2020). Rosalyn, an undergraduate student, was impressed that her instructor not only learned her name but remembered several other facts about her that she had shared during an introductory activity (Harrington, 2021). McFarlane (2023) highlighted the importance of learning to pronounce students' names correctly. Asking students to make recordings of the correct pronunciation of their names can be helpful in this regard. Mispronouncing names or using nicknames can be highly detrimental to a student who might perceive they are not worth the instructor's time and energy (Kohli & Solórzano, 2012). Moore et al. (2020) noted that names carry ancestral significance in some cultures.

Language is powerfully connected to identity (Cooper et al., 2020). Using names and pronouns that students have shared affirms those students and creates a conducive space for them to share more about themselves (Álvarez, 2022). It is important to keep in mind that the name and pronoun a student shares with their instructor may not be the one they want to be used in the classroom or with others. It is therefore advisable for instructors to ask each student where they would like their name and pronoun to be used.

Helping students incorporate their student role into their identity is also important. For example, calling the students "scholars" can help them internalize their new student role into their existing identity (Blackstone, 2013). Using future-focused career terminology can also help students discover their emerging professional identities (Rendón Linares & Muñoz, 2011). For example, if Kwame wants to be a judge, the instructor might consider referring to him as Future Judge Kwame or Justice Kwame. This strategy can empower and motivate the student. It can also help students develop a stronger connection with their instructor because it demonstrates that the instructor has been listening and honoring their goals as well as their desires. Even more importantly, it communicates that the instructor believes in them.

Strategy 3: Meet with Students Individually

One important way that instructors can convey their care is by inviting learners to meet with them outside of class, perhaps during student hours. There is some promising assessment data on the positive impact of this strategy. For example, Oakton Community College initiated a Persistence Project on their campus that asked instructors to arrange a 15-minute meeting with every student in at least one of their classes. These meetings focused on getting to know the students and improving the instructors' understanding of their needs. The findings were encouraging. The persistence rate for students of instructors who participated in the project was

65.7 percent from Fall 2017 to Fall 2018, compared to 51.4 percent for students of instructors who did not participate. In other words, students who met with at least one instructor outside of class were more likely to stay in school. Although this approach benefited all of those involved, it was especially beneficial for the Black participants, whose persistence rate from Fall 2017 to Fall 2018 was 60.7 percent, compared to just 42.2 percent for those with no instructors in the project (Supiano, 2020).

Instructors might consider asking the following questions during these meetings:

- What pronouns do you use, and do you have a preferred name?
- Why did you decide to attend college?
- What are your career aspirations?
- Which subject, class, or course do you like the most? Why?
- Which subject, class, or course do you like the least? Why?
- When you do well in class, how would you like to be recognized? In class? Privately? Would you like me to share your success with someone you care about?
- Who do you look up to? Who are your role models?
- What are your favorite foods, places to go, or things to do?
- When did you enjoy learning the most and why?
- What educator made an impact on you? How?
- How do people earn your respect or love?

Although this strategy of individual meetings can be highly effective, it may not be appropriate for your institution due to capacity issues. Meeting with students individually can be very time-consuming. Instructors could consult with their department chairperson and ask if they can allocate some class time to meeting with students individually. Perhaps groups could work on a project and instructors could hold brief individual meetings while this is happening. If instructors cannot connect with each student for 15 minutes, perhaps they could find just 5 minutes per student before or after class.

Strategies to Use throughout the Semester to Nurture Relationships

Building rapport in the classroom and intentionally fostering instructor–student and student–student connections at the start of the semester is important. It is equally important, however, for instructors to continue creating a sense of community and belonging throughout the semester. As instructors develop a more in-depth understanding of their students, they can modify assignments or assist students with seeing how best to leverage assignment options to build on their cultural strengths and develop the skills they need to achieve their goals.

Strategy 1: Explain How Assignments Connect to Personal and Professional Lives

Transparency provides students with more information about their learning activities and why they are doing them (see Chapter 7). The intention behind increased transparency is to make learning activities more meaningful to students, as this leads to increased motivation and more successful learning outcomes (Kirkpatrick, 2020). The TILT (Transparency in Learning and Technology) framework, developed by Dr. Mary-Ann Winkelmes and colleagues, provides techniques and strategies to help instructors share the "why" and "what" of what students are being asked to do (Winkelmes et al., 2016). Instructors using the TILT approach need to think continually about how to make assignment requirements more transparent for their students. First, instructors can communicate the purpose of an assignment or activity. The more instructors know about their students, the easier it will be for them to make specific connections between learning tasks and their personal and professional lives. For example, an instructor could explain that a group project will enable the students to learn how to work well in a team, benefit from diverse perspectives, and learn about the topic or focus of the group work. If an instructor knows that a student is interested in international business, they can articulate how these skills will be useful in that specific field. For adult students who are already working in the field, the instructor can point out ways that the skills learned during a group project can be put into action immediately in their current position.

Validating a student's culture through culturally affirming and meaningful assignments is an important aspect of creating an inclusive and welcoming learning environment. Students come from diverse cultural backgrounds with a variety of perspectives, and they bring their own cultural strengths to their learning (Yosso, 2016). Instructors can make efforts to validate a student's culture by making connections between their experiences and backgrounds and the content or skills being learned. When instructors incorporate relevant materials and culturally affirming examples into instructional approaches and assignments, this demonstrates that they value the student's culture and helps the student to feel validated in their own identity.

Instructors can also embrace and use student work products as examples to motivate others (Kunjufu, 2009), but they must ensure that these examples represent the diversity of the student body. After receiving permission to do so, they can showcase the work students have created. Most students find examples and models to be useful and supportive of their learning (see Chapter 8). However, it is important to be mindful that not every student will feel comfortable in the spotlight, perhaps because they have not experienced many positive affirmations in the past. Therefore, instructors should have conversations with students about how best to recognize them for their work.

Strategy 2: Provide Ongoing Culturally Affirming Support throughout the Semester

Throughout the semester, it is helpful for instructors to allocate time to regular check-ins. This strategy not only shows students that instructors care about them and their progress toward their goals but also helps instructors gauge if students are on track or if they would benefit from additional support. Students can be encouraged to arrange meetings with their instructors during student hours, or instructors can check in on students before or after each class period. For online classes, emails or direct messages can be a great way for instructors to stay connected with students and find out how they are doing.

Whole-class announcements about upcoming assignments can be another means of connecting learning tasks to students' current experiences and explaining how the knowledge and skills learned will be useful as they pursue their personal and professional aspirations. Such announcements and emails can be pre-scheduled so that instructors can set up a series of just-in-time messages without having to remember to do this throughout the semester.

In addition to checking in on academic progress, instructors can send congratulations on personal accomplishments or celebratory notes on special occasions, such as birthdays or holidays, if the student's culture observes them. Instructors should also be mindful of holidays when setting due dates for assignments. Flexibility is a culturally affirming approach. Students will appreciate it if their instructor recognizes that their priority may need to shift away from school during an important holiday or other special occasion.

Conclusion

Getting to know students is a critical first step in creating culturally affirming and meaningful assignments. Instructors who build and nurture relationships with their students will know how to create and modify assignments so that they are more culturally affirming and meaningful. They will also know how to help students see the current and future value of assignments. Instructors can take actions before the semester even begins to get to know their students by reviewing institutional demographic data and conducting student surveys. Focusing on developing strong instructor–student and student–student connections on day one and early in the semester is also important, and many different activities and assignments can be used for this purpose. Instructors can then continue to nurture these relationships throughout the semester. All these actions will help instructors set assignments that students perceive as culturally affirming and meaningful.

Reflection Questions

1. In what ways do you learn about your students before the start of the semester?
2. What is your positionality and how does this impact what assignments you create and how you teach?
3. What is your teaching philosophy and how do you communicate it to your students?
4. How do you introduce yourself to your students or help your students get to know you?
5. How do your introductory course documents help students get to know you and what is expected of them in the course?
6. Which first-day class activities will help you learn about your students and help them connect to you and their classmates?
7. How do you use ongoing communication tools to stay connected to students, help students see the relevance of learning tasks, and determine what additional support students might need during assignments?

References

Álvarez, B. (2022, October 5). Why pronouns matter. *NEA Today*. https://www.nea.org/advocating-for-change/new-from-nea/why-pronouns-matter.

Blackstone, J. (2013). At California school, twin principals are better than one. *CBS News*. https://www.cbsnews.com/news/at-california-school-twin-principals-are-better-than-one/.

Bonem, E. M., Fedesco, H. N., & Zissimopoulos, A. N. (2020). What you do is less important than how you do it: The effects of learning environment on student outcomes. *Learning Environments Research*, 23, 27–44. doi:10.1007/s10984-019-09289-8.

Buskirk-Cohen, A. A., & Plants, A. (2019). Caring about success: Students' perceptions of professors' caring matters more than grit. *International Journal of Teaching and Learning in Higher Education*, 31(1), 108–114.

Chun, E., & Evans, A. (2019). *Conducting an institutional diversity audit in higher education: A practitioner's guide to systematic diversity transformation*. Routledge.

Cooper, K. M. et al. (2020). Fourteen recommendations to create a more inclusive environment for LGBTQ+ individuals in academic biology. *CBE Life Sciences Education*, 19(3). https://doi.org/10.1187/cbe.20-04-0062.

Demir, M., Burton, S., & Dunbar, N. (2019). Professor–student rapport and perceived autonomy support as predictors of course and student outcomes. *Teaching of Psychology*, 46(1), 22–33.

Flanigan, A. E., Akcaoglu, M., & Ray, E. (2022). Initiating and maintaining student–instructor rapport in online classes. *The Internet and Higher Education*, 53, 1–11. doi:10.1016/j.iheduc.2021.100844.

Gehlbach, H., Brinkworth, M. E., King, A. M., Hsu, L. M., McIntyre, J., & Rogers, T. (2016). Creating birds of similar feathers: Leveraging similarity to improve teacher–student relationships and academic achievement. *Journal of Educational Psychology*, 108(3), 342–352.

Harrington, C. (2021). *Keeping us engaged: Student perspectives (and research-based strategies) on what works and why*. Routledge.

Harrington, C. (2022, January 26). Reflect on your positionality to ensure student success. *Inside Higher Ed*. https://www.insidehighered.com/advice/2022/01/26/successful-instructors-understand-their-own-biases-and-beliefs-opinion.

Harrington, C., & Thomas, M. (2018). *Designing a motivational syllabus: Creating a learning path for student engagement*. Routledge.

Hegarty, N. (2015). The growing importance of teaching philosophy statements and what they mean for the future: Why teaching philosophy statements will affect you. *Journal of Adult Education*, 44(2), 28–30.

Hernandez, P. (2021). *The pedagogy of real talk: Engaging, teaching, and connecting with students at-promise*. Corwin Press.

Kirkpatrick, M. (2020, February 27). Transparency in the classroom. JMU Center for Faculty Innovation. https://www.jmu.edu/cfi/_files/t-t_19-20/02.27.20-transparency-in-the-classroom.pdf.

Kohli, R. & Solórzano, D. G. (2012). Teachers, please learn our names! Racial microaggressions and the K-12 classroom. *Race Ethnicity and Education*, 15(4), 441–462, doi:10.1080/13613324.2012.674026.

Kunjufu, J. (2009). *200+ educational strategies to teach children of color*. African American Images.

Laundon, M., Cathcart, A., & Greer, D. A. (2020). Teaching philosophy statements. *Journal of Management Education*, 44(5), 577–587. doi:10.1177/1052562920942289.

Legg, A. M., & Wilson, J. H. (2009). E-mail from professor enhances student motivation and attitudes. *Teaching of Psychology*, 36(3), 205–211. doi:10.1080/00986280902960034.

Levin, R. (2018). The problem with pronouns. *Inside Higher Ed*. https://www.insidehighered.com/views/2018/09/19/why-asking-students-their-preferred-pronoun-not-good-idea-opinion.

Liao, M., Lewis, G., & Winiski, M. (2020). Do students learn better with Pecha Kucha, an alternative presentation format? *Journal of Microbiology and Biology Education*, 21(3), 6. doi:10.1128/jmbe.v21i3.2111.

McFarlane, L. (2023, July 17). Why pronouncing student names correctly matters, and how to get them right. *Education Week*. https://www.edweek.org/leadership/why-pronouncing-student-names-correctly-matters-and-how-to-get-them-right/2023/07.

Moore, L. L., Stewart, M. L., Slanda, D. D., Placencia, A., & Moore, M. M. (2020). The power of a name: Nontraditional names, teacher efficacy, and expected learning outcomes. *Journal of English Learner Education*, 11(1), 83–103.

Muñiz, J. (2020, September 23). Culturally responsive teaching: A reflection guide. New America. https://www.newamerica.org/education-policy/policy-papers/culturally-responsive-teaching-competencies/.

Museus, S. D., Yi, V., & Saelua, N. (2017). The impact of culturally engaging campus environments on sense of belonging. *Review of Higher Education*, 40(2), 187–215. https://doi.org/10.1353/rhe.2017.0001.

Pecha Kucha (n.d.). What is a 20×20 PechaKucha?https://www.pechakucha.com/.

Pedersen, P. (2004). *110 experiences for multicultural learning*. American Psychological Association.

Pinder-Grover, T., Green, K. R., & Millunchick, J. M. (2011). The efficacy of screencasts to address the diverse academic needs of students in a large lecture course. *Advances in Engineering Education*, 2(3), 1–28.

Rendón Linares, L. I., & Muñoz, S. M. (2011). Revisiting validation theory: Theoretical foundations, applications, and extensions. *Enrollment Management Journal*, 5, 12–33.

Ruffini, M. (2012, October 31). Screencasting to engage learning. *Educause Review*. https://er.educause.edu/articles/2012/11/screencasting-to-engage-learning.

Schlossberg, N. K. (1989). Marginality and mattering: Key issues in building community. *New Directions for Student Services*, 48, 5–15. doi:10.1002/ss.37119894803.

Steele, C. (2011). *Whistling Vivaldi: How stereotypes affect us and what we can do*. W. W. Norton & Company.

Supiano, B. (2020, February 7). To improve persistence, this college asks professors to have a 15-minute meeting with each student. *Chronicle of Higher Education*. https://www.chronicle.com/newsletter/teaching/2020-02-06?cid2=gen_login_refresh&cid=gen_sign_in.

Taylor, E., Tisdell, E., & Stone Hanley, M. (2000). The role of positionality in teaching for critical consciousness: Implications for adult education. In *Adult Education Research Conference 2000 conference proceedings (Vancouver, BC, Canada)* (pp. 1–8). New Prairie Press. https://newprairiepress.org/cgi/viewcontent.cgi?referer=&httpsredir=1&article=2228&context=aerc.

Virtue, E. E., Root, B., & Lenner, R. (2021). Appreciative advising as a mechanism for student development. *College Student Affairs Journal*, 39(2), 200–213. doi:10.1353/csj.2021.0017.

White, K. E., Harris, P. F., & Wood, J. L. E. (2015). *Teaching men of color in the community college: A guidebook*. Montezuma Publishing.

Winkelmes, M., Bernacki, M., Butler, J., Zochowski, M., Golanics, J., & Weavil, K. H. (2016). A teaching intervention that increases underserved college students' success. *Peer Review*, 18(1), 31–36. https://www.proquest.com/docview/1805184428.

Yosso, T. J. (2016). Whose culture has capital? In A. D. Dixson, C. K. Rousseau Anderson, & J. K. Donnor (Eds.), *Critical race theory in education* (pp. 113–136). Routledge. http://dx.doi.org/10.4324/9781315709796-7.

Chapter 5

Exploring Assignment Options beyond the Exam

James K. Winfield

Nakia, a Black female student, is sitting down to take her final exam in her first engineering course. Although she has studied every day for the past two weeks, she is quite anxious. She looks around the room and sees that there are only a few women in the class and most of the students are White. She begins to question whether she belongs in the engineering field. Nakia really wants to show the world that she can do this, but she has heard repeatedly that men are better than women at math. She has also seen many of her Black friends, men and women, who started as engineering majors change their major because it was "too hard." Her anxiety continues to rise as her professor hands out the exam.

Nakia found this exam to be quite stressful. The final exam is one of the most commonly used summative assignments in college. Summative assignments, which are typically due at the end of a course or unit, have long been used as a tried-and-true practice to gauge students' finite understanding of concepts in a course. They provide an opportunity for students to demonstrate that they have achieved the course learning outcomes. In many college courses, summative assignments come in the form of multiple-choice exams and research papers, and they are often developed with the lens of capturing a specific answer rather than allowing room for creativity and personal and cultural connection (Stoerger, 2018; Singer-Freeman et al., 2019). It is common for summative assignments to require students to rely on memorization and information regurgitation, which studies have shown does not always create a pleasurable learning experience (Stoerger, 2018).

There is some evidence that instructors are not requiring exams as much as they did previously. Findings from a descriptive study revealed that 67 percent of the psychology syllabi from 1999 to 2005 that were reviewed required non-cumulative exams, compared to only 46 percent of psychology syllabi from 2016 to 2022. Similarly, final exams have been less commonly used or required in recent years. These developments were found to be statistically significant, though the effect size was small (Harrington, 2023). Despite this shift, however, exams and research papers continue to be among the most frequently used assignment requirements (Harrington, 2023).

DOI: 10.4324/9781003443797-6

Challenges Associated with Traditional Assignments

Traditional assignments, such as exams, often perpetuate equity gaps. There is a long history of research illustrating that tests and exams are biased (Rosales & Walker, 2021), and as a result, students from different cultural backgrounds often perform differently in exams even if their ability levels are similar. For example, Singer-Freeman et al. (2019) reported substantial equity gaps in exam performance between students from underrepresented minority groups and their peers. Specifically, in the theatre appreciation course that was studied, the average scores on a multiple-choice exam were 69 for students from underrepresented minority groups and 82 for other students. When the same students were asked to complete an inclusive writing assignment instead of an exam, the equity gap in performance was minimal, with students from underrepresented minority groups earning an average grade of 88 and other students earning an average grade of 93 (Singer-Freeman et al., 2019).

The negative impact of exams extends beyond performance in courses. In an extensive study and review of high school exit exams conducted by New America, Hystop (2014, p. 6) reported that "high school exit exams nationwide had not increased student achievement, but rather decreased graduation rates by two percentage points, on average." Referring to students with disabilities who may need accommodations such as extra time or the option of sitting the exam in a low-distraction environment, Saucier et al. (2022) argued that it can be "stigmatizing for those students to be unable to take the exam with their classmates and they may feel their absences are conspicuous."

Many scholars have questioned if exams measure the knowledge and skills described in the course learning outcomes and those that are needed in the world of work. Davis (2022), for instance, questioned whether asking students to complete a task in a timed situation without any resources mirrors what will be expected in the workplace and argued that students should have access to their notes during exams. Similarly, Bengtsson (2019, p. 2) advocated for take-home exams as they are often more challenging and require students to "retrieve, apply, and synthesize information"—higher-level cognitive skills that students will need when they begin their careers.

There are many reasons why traditional assignments such as exams and research papers are problematic. First, research has illustrated that testing bias can disadvantage students of color, students from low-income households, and students from marginalized backgrounds (Fuentes et al., 2020). In addition, exams are likely to trigger stereotype threat. According to Steele (2010), if a member of a group with a negative stereotype faces a high-stakes performance task, such as an exam, they are likely to experience anxiety about confirming the stereotype. This may lead to poor performance in comparison with students who are members of groups with positive stereotypes, even when the members of the two groups have similar abilities (Steele, 2010). It is likely that Nakia, the Black female student taking the final exam in her engineering class, experienced stereotype threat. Moreover, another study found that students of color and other students from marginalized groups often have higher levels of test anxiety than their peers, which can also contribute to lower scores in exams (Hardacre et al., 2021).

Traditional research papers, which are still commonly used (Harrington, 2023), may not help students develop the writing skills they will need in their careers. Although they provide opportunities for students to develop their written communication skills, which are highly valued by employers (Korostoff, 2020), academic writing is very different from the type of writing they will most likely use in the workplace. For example, business writing is often more flexible and collaborative in nature (Boogaard, n.d.). Ranaut (2018, p. 32) identified numerous skills associated with effective business writing, such as that "the writing should be practical, factual, concise, clear, and persuasive." In business, workers are often required to express their ideas succinctly in a one-page document, rather than a 10- or 20-page research paper, so it is important to help students develop these skills (Wright & Larsen, 2016).

Another challenge with traditional research papers is that instructors often require students to rely exclusively or primarily on peer-reviewed research articles. This can be problematic in terms of inclusivity. Although academic journals rarely collect data on the racial and gender identities of their authors and reviewers, there is some evidence that there is little diversity among those who review and publish journal articles. For instance, Wu (2020) reported that 75–80 percent of scientific journals' authors and reviewers who provided racial or gender information identified as White males, whereas fewer than 10 percent identified as Black, Latino, Indigenous, or Native. While Wu acknowledged that this sample represented only 10–20 percent of the journals' total contributors, her findings suggest that peer-reviewed articles are unlikely to be representative of diverse authorship.

Unfortunately, traditional assignments can usually be characterized as a one-size-fits-all approach to teaching practice (Varsavsky & Rayner, 2013). "There is an assumption at play within the field of assessment that while there are multiple ways for students to learn, students need to demonstrate learning in specific ways for it to count" (Montenegro & Jankowski, 2017, p. 6). To make learning more engaging, equitable, and applicable, other methods and practices should be prioritized in the classroom. Projects and assignments that lean into real-world experiences, encourage collaboration, and emphasize skills should be the new norm (Wollschleger, 2019). More innovative, project-based summative assignments, when provided as options or required, can lead to much better outcomes (Singer-Freeman et al., 2019).

Unique assessments that encourage students to connect their personal experiences and prior learning to the curriculum can foster a deeper understanding of a subject or concepts (Zakrajsek, 2022). As facilitators of learning, instructors should measure knowledge and skills practically and equitably. Using alternative forms of assessments and assignments will not only counteract the inherent bias of traditional assessments (Singer-Freeman et al., 2019) but also create learning opportunities that are more culturally affirming (see Chapter 2). Referring back to Nakia's story, she likely would have appreciated an opportunity to showcase her knowledge in a less stressful way than an exam. Moreover, her performance on an alternative assignment probably would have provided a more accurate reflection of what she had learned.

Alternative Summative Assessments

Students have reported appreciating the opportunity to complete innovative and creative assessments (Harrington, 2021). Varsavsky and Rayner (2013) conducted a study with science students that showed greater satisfaction among those who participated in an alternative assessment as opposed to a traditional exam. The alternative assessment in question was a practical lab project that incorporated collaborative analysis of findings. George and Thompson (2024) highlighted the importance of choice when developing culturally affirming assignments. In addition, the students in Varsavsky and Rayner's (2013) study praised the alternative assessment method because it sparked creativity and reflection, whereas the traditional exam limited creative expression.

Varsavsky and Rayner's (2013) research substantiated the need for diverse assessments and made the case for constructivism in modern learning. Wasson (1996) posited that constructivist theory should foster a flexible process and framework of learning that is less rigid in its conventions. When designing equitable learning environments, facilitators of learning must consider the meaning and purpose of each assignment and how the diverse students in the class may respond to the learning tasks, given their varied cultural backgrounds and lived experiences (see Chapter 3).

Yosso (2005) urged educators to adopt culturally affirming learning practices that allow students to see themselves in their work and apply what they are learning to their lived experiences. Conceição and Howles (2021) also discussed the importance of learning design and how culture, ethnicity, and gender are vital pillars to consider when designing courses and assignments. Diversifying course assignment options can lead to increased satisfaction and connection to content (Garner, 2012; Flinders & Thornton, 2017). Alternative assignments also often make more room for higher-order thinking and provide more opportunities to create, which is the highest tier in Bloom's revised taxonomy (Anderson & Krathwohl, 2001).

Although a ten-page paper might illustrate a student's grasp of writing conventions and their ability to expand upon a subject, and an exam might enable them to demonstrate the knowledge they have gained, other assignments can be equally effective at capturing mastery of course learning outcomes. This is not to say that exams and research papers should never be used. In some cases, especially in fields that require formal testing for entry into the workplace, it can be very important for instructors to prepare their students through examination. However, instructors are also encouraged to consider the many ways in which learning outcomes could be assessed, rather than relying exclusively on traditional assignments merely because of historical precedent. Several of these alternative assessment methods are discussed below.

Infographics

Infographics, as the name suggests, involves the presentation of information in graphic form (Toth, 2013). The technique was first used in the philanthropy and business sectors to highlight data or processes (Toth, 2013; Stoerger, 2018), but it has since made its way into classrooms, with some instructors allowing students to use it to demonstrate what they have learned. For example, Lorraine Cella allows her students to choose an infographic format from a list of options for a memoir assignment in a writing course (see Appendix, Example 13).

Infographic assignments can foster many essential skills that can prove useful in the workplace. For instance, students will develop analysis skills when working on an infographic assignment. In addition, this type of assignment enables students to practice writing persuasively and succinctly and communicating key concepts in a visually compelling and attractive layout. Students who create infographics will need to determine how to showcase key data points and communicate information in a visually effective way. This includes determining which icons, images, and graphics best convey the most important content.

There are many different types of infographics and numerous ways to create them. Therefore, the instructor should consider providing an overview of the approach as well as several examples. Murray and Scafe (Chapter 8) emphasize the importance of providing models or examples to scaffold student learning. Ideally, instructors should share several examples rather than just one in order to demonstrate the varied ways in which information can be communicated. It is hoped that this will spark creativity among the students, and mean that they will not have to fit their content into a prescribed template.

Instructors may find it useful to share their knowledge of technology resources to support students' acquisition of the skills they need to create effective infographics. Technological platforms like Piktochart, Canva, and DesignCap are just a few of the low-cost or free options. Navigation of these platforms' user-friendly templates and tutorials typically requires minimal expertise (University of Michigan LSA Learning & Teaching Consultants, n.d.).

Infographic projects may be completed either independently or collaboratively with other students. This type of process choice is encouraged by George and Thompson in Chapter 6.

One-Pagers, Executive Summaries, or Policy Briefs

Most professional writing is succinct, yet, in academic settings, students are often asked to write lengthy papers. "The ability to write in a concise fashion is a useful skill for students with future careers in government, business, nonprofits, journalism, electoral politics, or even academia" (McMillan, 2014, p. 109). In business and the nonprofit sector, for example, employees are often asked to write executive summaries, one-pagers, or policy briefs to convey key concepts, data, and metrics. These brief, visually effective documents enable busy professionals to take in the key points quickly and use the data to inform decision-making.

Requiring students to write executive summaries, one-pagers, or briefs is a good way to help them develop the writing skills they will need in the workplace while they are learning essential course content (Wright & Larsen, 2016). McMillan (2014) argued that writing succinctly can be more cognitively challenging than writing longer papers because students need to think critically about what information is most important and what to include. Findings from a research study that evaluated the writing skills of students completing a series of one-pager assignments in a marketing class indicated that writing errors significantly declined and the quality of the writing improved over the course of the semester, especially among students who were identified as weak writers at the start of the class (Wright & Larsen, 2016). An added benefit of this approach is that instructor grading time is reduced when written products are more succinct (Wright & Larsen, 2016). One concern that instructors may have with succinctly written products is that students may "shy away from significant research" with a briefer assignment, but this can be addressed by requiring students to include numerous resources and a works cited page, and working through the steps of creating this type of written product (McMillan, 2014, p. 111).

Pecha Kucha Presentations

There are various iterations of quick presentations. One such is Pecha Kucha, a fast-paced presentation method that relies on images rather than text. In a Pecha Kucha presentation, students must convey their message in just 20 slides, with each slide displayed for only 20 seconds (Qin et al., 2022; Carroll et al., 2016). This prioritizes the major points of the presentation and conveys the major ideas using images rather than words on the slides (Carroll et al., 2016). Pecha Kuchas can be done virtually or in person, and instructors can modify the 20 slides × 20 seconds per slide rule to fit their needs. For example, if an instructor wanted each student to present a Pecha Kucha in 5 minutes, students could be instructed to use 15 slides at 20 seconds per slide.

It is important to recognize that it takes time for students to develop content expertise and prepare for a presentation, especially if the format is new to them. Instructors can consider providing videos or other resources in the learning management system or allocating class time for students to prepare for or practice their presentations. Instructors may also want to consider initiating a peer-feedback process while the presentation is being developed. Allocating class time may be even more important for group-format presentations, as this will remove the barrier of having to find a time that works for all students in the group. It can also be helpful to provide presentation preparation tips to students. Qin et al. (2022) reported that students found faculty input and support useful.

The University of Illinois Urbana–Champaign School of Information Sciences (n.d.) offered the following tips for students preparing a Pecha Kucha presentation:

- Focus on one central point or idea.
- Use images and limit the use of words.
- Construct a script and rehearse the presentation.

Engaging in brief presentations such as Pecha Kuchas helps students build essential presentation skills while showing their mastery of content knowledge, themes, and information. Research has shown that this type of presentation style can reduce cognitive load for students and allow them to focus on the content they are learning and communicating (Qin et al., 2022). Identifying and sharing key points and data in a short period of time in a visually effective way is a skill that will prove useful in the workplace as most employers will ask their employees to convey even complex ideas in brief presentation formats.

Media-Based Assignments: Podcasts and Videos

A growing modality in learning is the use of multimedia resources, which includes employing audio and visual means to hear and see experts, peers, and thought leaders in a specific content area. According to Adams et al. (2021), podcasting encompasses both listening to and creating podcasts. These products, which often comprise informal interviews, can be an impactful way to start or continue dialogues on causes, issues, or practices (Adams et al., 2021). Rogers (2021) asserted that they are a versatile and authentic assessment option and noted that video sources, whether they are watched, created, or referenced, can be a creative way for students to learn and articulate their comprehension of course content.

The benefits of podcasting and other media projects, including creating videos or screencasts, go beyond helping students master course content. Students who create podcasts can also enhance their technical skills because recording them requires the use of software and other technology tools. In addition, students can build and strengthen their professional networks as they will identify and interview content experts in the field. When students are assigned to work on these media projects in small groups, they can also enhance their collaboration skills as they are exposed to diverse ideas and perspectives. Thus, technical and essential skills that will be useful in the world of work can be developed through this type of assignment (see Chapter 3).

Students have reported believing that creative podcasts have value in the college curriculum (McCarthy et al., 2023). Specifically, the average student response to a question about whether it is useful to include podcasting in the curriculum was 4.26 on a 5.0 Likert scale, with 5 indicating "strongly agree." These findings show that students find value and meaning in assignments that incorporate multimedia.

Social Media Posts or Blogs

Social media is an excellent way for students to express their thoughts and ideas publicly:

> Social media is used so widely. Since so many cultural, political, and social discourses are occurring online, students need to know how to use SM in a way that is productive to society and their education, not just for entertainment purposes.
>
> (Kester & Vie, 2019, p. 61)

Iloh (2018) argued that social media is an important type of public scholarship, so students should be assisted with developing their use of it as a skill.

There are many opportunities for students to explore cultural issues and engage in advocacy via social media channels. For example, they can craft social media posts that provide insights, expand knowledge, and issue calls for action. Students may be asked to develop a series of posts or a social media campaign to raise awareness of a subject they are studying in class. This type of assignment can have an impact locally, nationally, or even globally, with the result that students perceive it as culturally affirming and meaningful (see Chapters 2 and 3). For example, a student may raise awareness of underserved populations, food insecurity, access to healthcare, or financial literacy. A social media assignment can therefore empower students to use their knowledge in an authentic, meaningful, and culturally affirming way.

Social media assignments fall into what Kester and Vie (2019) term "critical digital pedagogy," which encourages students to use their writing skills in a relatable manner on platforms that are widely accessed. For example, students in a writing composition course might be asked to share prose, poetry, or drama on social media (Kester & Vie, 2019). Rosinski (2017) noted that an effective strategy to integrate social media is to help students see their current strengths and experiences with writing in a social media format and then stretch them to consider professional outlets for sharing the knowledge and expertise they are gaining.

Another way to empower students to curate their content is to ask them to write a blog or opinion piece based on an experience or concept they have learned. Asking students to reflect on content learned from various readings and other course materials, as well as their own lived experiences, is a good way for instructors to be culturally affirming (see Chapter 2). Research has shown that students appreciate the benefits of this approach. For example, in a study of an introductory economics course, Cameron (2012) found that 91.5 percent of students who were actively engaged in blogging attributed their ability to apply economics in the real world to their engagement with the blogs. Students are often motivated by assignments that are shared publicly (see Chapter 3).

Book Reviews

Book reviews provide students with opportunities to analyze texts that they find particularly interesting. In a study conducted by Preuss et al. (2013), students stressed that they should be able to choose the texts they read for book review assignments. They also noted that such assignments, which require them to discover and write about at least three course-related concepts, help them understand course content and its real-world applications. A further benefit of book review assignments is that they encourage students to engage in public scholarship. When students publish their reviews, people in the field can read their perspectives on the resource in question (Kezar et al., 2018).

Book reviews should focus on reflection and implications rather than merely reciting the book's themes. Strategic question prompts can help students stretch themselves cognitively to see connections between the concepts they are learning in class and what is being discussed in the book. Students can also be encouraged to engage in critical analysis of the book, identifying strengths and where the text may have fallen short.

Instructors can encourage students to share their book reviews in a variety of modalities. Too often, book reviews and other assignments are transactional, between instructor and student, yet others would benefit from reading or hearing the latter's perspectives, too. Encouraging students to share their work in creative and public ways can be beneficial to both the student and the field. Marable et al. (2010), for example, highlighted the value of a book talk or discussion group assignment in which undergraduate students discussed a book related to course content that focused on understanding the challenges of individuals with disabilities. The students found value in hearing the perspectives of others, sharing their thoughts and ideas, and clarifying concepts that were not initially clear. They also reported gaining a better understanding of the course content and developed greater empathy for individuals with disabilities after completing the assignment.

Experiential Learning Assignments

Internships are a great way to increase students' understanding of a field while also supporting their employability (Dacre Pool & Sewell, 2007). Although internship opportunities may not be available to students until later in their academic journeys, instructors can use assignments in courses to expose students to careers and help them develop essential career skills. For example, they can invite guests to attend a career panel and require students to conduct informational interviews. These opportunities enrich the students' understanding of the field of study. The assignment can then be a reflective one in which students respond to several question prompts either in writing or orally. When identifying and recommending individuals for a panel or interviews, instructors are encouraged to consider the diversity of the professionals. Diversity in age, race and ethnicity, gender, country of origin, and experience would add value to the narratives and allow students to connect with and see themselves and others represented in the workforce.

Another experiential learning assignment option is workplace simulation. Ismail and Sabapathy (2016) defined this as a form of project-based learning in which the classroom is considered as a workplace and the students treat each other as colleagues as they work together toward the assignment goal. For example, at the National University in Singapore, students were required to create a website and logo, draft communications from the CEO to management, organize professional development events and workshops, and request updates via presentations for the board of directors (Ismail & Sabapathy, 2016).

Workplace simulations can help orient students to the world of work while developing the essential skills they will need in the workplace. Ismail and Sabapathy (2016) noted that skill development occurred because the norms, behaviors, and expectations of the workspace were mirrored. Simulation activities provide students with opportunities to experiment with skills and content (Kolb, 1984). The experiential learning cycle is beneficial because students directly interact—and wrestle—with real-life challenges (Howard, 2015).

Researchers (Ismail & Sabapathy, 2016) have found that students perceive simulation assignments to be valuable, engaging, and practical, with the experience characterized as more refreshing than traditional assessments. Some students even stated that the experience gave them insights into what to expect in the corporate world.

Training Manuals or Playbooks

Another innovative assignment idea is to have students create a playbook or training manual based on research, emerging trends, and discussions related to a content area. Training manuals or playbooks provide employees with succinct summaries of essential job-related content and guidance on suggested practices or actions. Because these resources are often used in the professional world, students will immediately see the value of such assignments. The creation of a playbook or training manual can help students synthesize learning and articulate processes and policies. It also puts students in the driver's seat in terms of content sharing, as they will have the autonomy to format and design their findings in a way that is appealing to the intended population, profession, or community. Thus, training manuals or playbooks help students gain a deep knowledge of course content while also providing them with opportunities to practice synthesis and the communication of key concepts to the target audience in a user-friendly way.

An example of a training manual or playbook assignment could be in an education course, where students must identify a sub-population of students and how to support them in the classroom. A student who chooses neurodivergent children might reference emergent trends to share best practices that practitioners can utilize in their classrooms as they seek to be more aware of the vast sensory needs of their students and how to make accommodations for neurodiversity.

It can be useful to require students to write a reflective essay or statement about the process of developing a training manual or playbook (Harvard University Derek Bok Center for Teaching and Learning, n.d.). The addition of a reflective component to the assignment enables students to focus on the process as well as the content. Reflecting on process skills can help students refine skills that they will need in the future.

Formative Assessments

In addition to considering alternatives to traditional summative assessments, it is important to provide students with opportunities to learn from formative assessments throughout the course. Instructors are encouraged to incorporate more varied options of formative assessments into their courses. Examples of formative assessments are quizzes, drafts of work, online discussions, and sections of a summative assignment. A recent study of psychology syllabi found that formative assessments have been used more frequently in recent years, yet fewer than half of the syllabi reviewed required students to complete formative assessments (Harrington, 2023). Thus, instructors still need to identify and use more formative assessments in their courses.

To reach the culmination of learning, there must be appropriate scaffolding to ensure that students can analyze, discover, and create meaning (Montenegro & Jankowski, 2017; see also Chapter 8). To fully evaluate student learning, an instructor can utilize an adaptive approach to gauge students' understanding and ability to apply various concepts throughout the semester, rather than waiting until grading a summative assessment product at the end of the unit or semester. Continued assessment of student learning can be accomplished by the intentional integration of experiences and the creation of various artifacts that showcase the students' understanding and identities (Garner, 2012; Singer-Freeman et al., 2019). Chapman and King (2005) posited that assignments could be leveraged as a means of information gathering to increase understanding of the learners. These ongoing assessments, whether informal or formal, are methods to determine interest, needs, prior learning, and dispositions that can inform the trajectory of engagement in an academic space (Chapman & King, 2005; Conceição & Howles, 2021). Students can modify their learning behaviors and instructors can adjust their teaching practices by using feedback from formative assessments. These modifications can lead to higher levels of learning and improved summative assessment products.

Conclusion

By diversifying all learning experiences, and especially assignments, instructors can create more inclusive learning environments where students feel empowered to innovate and apply their learning in creative ways (Montenegro & Jankowski, 2017). Garner (2012) emphasized the importance of enabling students to claim ownership over their learning experience, develop skills, and explore self and society—three pillars of constructivist ideals.

It is time for instructors to reimagine how assignments can be used to support the diverse learners in today's college classrooms and help them develop the skills they will need in the world of work (Garner, 2012; Singer-Freeman et al., 2019). Innovative assignments, such as those described in this chapter, can facilitate students' development of higher-order thinking (Anderson & Krathwohl, 2001) while also engaging them (Harrington, 2021). Although traditional assignments such as exams may still have value, especially when students need to pass standardized tests to gain entry into a particular career field, many alternative assignments have value, too. Therefore, instructors are encouraged to consider the many creative options that could provide evidence of students' attainment of course learning outcomes. The ideas discussed in this chapter, such as infographics, Pecha Kucha presentations, executive summaries, book reviews, and training manuals, are just a few of the possibilities for instructors to consider.

Reflection Questions

1. Who might benefit the most from traditional assignments such as exams and research papers? Who might not benefit from traditional assignments?
2. Why are you using traditional assignments (if you are) and what are the benefits of considering alternatives?
3. How would briefer assignments such as infographics, executive summaries, one-pagers, or policy briefs benefit your students and how do you (or could you) use this type of assignment in your class?
4. What types of media or social media assignments do you (or could you) use in your class and how could these be beneficial to your students?
5. How could you increase experiential learning opportunities in your class through assignments?
6. What type of alternative assignments would work best in your field and why?
7. What type of formative assessments do you currently use? How could you increase the number of formative assignments in your class?

References

Adams, K. *et al.* (2021, September 27). It's time for academe to take podcasting seriously. *Inside Higher Ed.* https://www.insidehighered.com/advice/2021/09/28/how-harness-podcasting-teaching-and-scholarship-opinion#:~:text=Assign%20scholarly%20podcasts%20as%20primary,podcasts%20should%20have%20written%20transcripts.

Anderson, L. W. & Krathwohl, D. R. (Eds.) (2001). *A taxonomy for learning, teaching, and assessing: A revision of Bloom's taxonomy of educational objectives* (complete ed.). Longman.

Bengtsson, L. (2019). Take-home exams in higher education: A systematic review. *Education Sciences*, 9, 1–16. doi:10.3390/educsci9040267.

Boogaard, K. (n.d.). Business writing vs. academic writing: What's the difference? *Go Skills*. https://www.goskills.com/Soft-Skills/Resources/Business-writing-vs-academic-writing.

Cameron, M. P. (2012). "Economics with training wheels": Using blogs in teaching and assessing introductory economics. *Journal of Economic Education*, 43(4), 397–407.

Carroll, A. J., Tchangalova, N., & Harrington, E. G. (2016). Flipping one-shot library instruction: Using Canvas and Pecha Kucha for peer teaching. *Journal of the Medical Library Association*, 104(2), 125–130.

Chapman, C., & King, R. (2005). *Differentiated assessment strategies. One tool does not fit all*. Corwin.

Conceição, S. C. O. & Howles, L. L. (2021). *Designing the online learning experience: Evidence-based principles and strategies*. Routledge.

Dacre Pool, L., & Sewell, P. (2007). The key to employability: Developing a practical model of graduate employability. *Education and Training*, 49(4), 277–289.

Davis, R. (2022, October 26). Opinion: Professors should consider giving open-note exams. *University Star*. https://www.universitystar.com/opinions/opinion-professors-should-consider-giving-open-note-exams/article_dedd8554-5552-11ed-94ee-83b3aed510a3.html.

Flinders, D. J., & Thornton, S. J. (2017). *The curriculum studies reader*. Routledge.

Fuentes, M. A., Zelaya, D. G., & Madsen, J. W. (2020). Rethinking the course syllabus: Considerations for promoting equity, diversity, and inclusion. *Teaching of Psychology*, 48(1), 69–79. doi:10.1.1177/0098628320959979.

Garner, B. (2012). *The first-year seminar: Designing, implementing, and assessing courses to support student learning and success*, Vol. 3: *Teaching in the first-year seminar*. Stylus Publishing.

Hardacre, B., Hafner, A., & Nakama, P. (2021). The impact of test anxiety on teacher credential candidates. *Teacher Education Quarterly*, 48(3), 7–28.

Harrington, C. (2021). *Keeping us engaged: Student perspectives (and research-based evidence) on what works and why*. Routledge.

Harrington, C. (2023). How much have assessments in psychology courses changed over time? A descriptive study. *Journal for Research and Practice in College Teaching*, 8(1), 1–14.

Harvard University Derek Bok Center for Teaching and Learning (n.d.). Assessing non-traditional assignments. https://bokcenter.harvard.edu/assessing-non-traditional-assignments.

Howard, J. R. (2015). *Discussion in the college classroom: Getting your students engaged and participating in person and online*. Jossey-Bass.

Hystop, A. (2014). The case against exit exams. New America Education. https://files.eric.ed.gov/fulltext/ED579082.pdf.

Iloh, C. (2018). Using social media as public scholarship. In A. J. Kezar, Y. Drivales, & J. A. Kitchen (Eds.), *Envisioning public scholarship for our time* (pp. 135–147). Routledge.

Ismail, N., & Sabapathy, C. (2016). Workplace simulation: An integrated approach to training university students in professional communication. *Business and Professional Communication Quarterly*, 79(4), 487–510.

Kester, J., & Vie, S. (2019). Social media in practice: Assignments, perceptions, possibilities. *Currents in Teaching and Learning*, 12(2), 52–70.

Kezar, A. J., Drivales, Y., & Kitchen, J. A. (Eds.) (2018). *Envisioning public scholarship for our time*. Routledge.

Kolb, D. A. (1984). *Experiential learning: Experience as the source of learning and development* (Vol. 1). Prentice-Hall.

Korostoff, K. (2020, September 4). Which skill do 82% of employers say they really want? Rockstar Research. https://www.researchrockstar.com/which-skill-do-82-of-employers-say-they-really-want/.

McCarthy, J., Porada, K., & Treat, R. (2023). Educational podcast impact on student study habits and exam performance. *Family Medicine*, 55(1), 34–37. doi:10.22454/FamMed.55.183124.

McMillan, S. L. (2014). Bravo for brevity: Using short paper assignments in international relations classes. *International Studies Perspectives*, 15(1), 109–120. doi:10.1111/insp.12003.

Marable, M. A., Leavitt-Noble, K., & Grande, M. (2010). Book talks in special education methods courses: Using literature to influence, inspire, and prepare teacher candidates. *Teacher Education and Special Education*, 33(2), 143–154.

Montenegro, E., & Jankowski, N. A. (2017, January). *Equity and assessment: Moving towards culturally responsive assessment*. University of Illinois and Indiana University, National Institute for Learning Outcomes Assessment.

Preuss, G. S., Schurtz, D. R., Powell, C. A. J., Combs, D. J. Y., & Smith, R. H. (2013). Connecting social psychology to the experience of others through a nonfiction book analysis: New wine in an old bottle. *Journal of the Scholarship of Teaching and Learning*, 13(2), 72–83.

Qin, H., Vaughan, B., Morley, P., & Ng, L. (2022). Peer teaching and Pecha Kucha for pharmacology. *The Clinical Teacher*, 19, 150–154.

Ranaut, B. (2018). Importance of good business writing skills. *International Journal of Language and Linguistics*, 5(2), 32–41. doi:10.30845/ijll.v5n2p3.

Rogers, H. (2021, July 30). Using podcasts in your classroom. Duke Learning Innovation. https://learninginnovation.duke.edu/blog/2021/07/using-podcasts-in-your-classroom/.

Rosales, J., & Walker, T. (2021, March 20). The racist beginnings of standardized testing. National Education Association. https://www.nea.org/advocating-for-change/new-from-nea/racist-beginnings-standardized-testing#:~:text=Since%20their%20inception%20almost%20a,from%20early%20childhood%20through%20college.

Rosinski, P. (2017). Students' perceptions of the transfer of rhetorical knowledge between digital self-sponsored writing and academic writing: The importance of authentic contexts and reflection. In J. L. Moore & C. M. Anson (Eds.), *Critical transitions: Writing and the question of transfer* (pp. 247–271). WAC Clearinghouse and University Press of Colorado.

Saucier, D. A., Renkin, N. D., & Schiffer, A. A. (2022, February 18). Five reasons to stop giving exams in class. *Faculty Focus*. https://www.facultyfocus.com/articles/educational-assessment/five-reasons-to-stop-giving-exams-in-class/.

Singer-Freeman, K. S., Hobbs, H., & Robinson, C. (2019). Theoretical matrix of culturally relevant assessment. *Assessment Update: Progress, Trends, and Practices in Higher Education*, 31(4), 1–16.

Steele, C. M. (2010). *Whistling Vivaldi: How stereotypes affect us and what we can do*. W. W. Norton & Company.

Stoerger, S. (2018). Writing without words: Designing for a visual learning experience. *Education for Information*, 34, 7–13.

Toth, C. (2013). Revisiting a genre: Teaching infographics in business and professional communication courses. *Business Communication Quarterly*, 76(4), 446–457.

University of Illinois Urbana–Champaign School of Information Sciences (n.d.). Presentation skills for librarians: Lightning talks. https://ischoolillinois.libguides.com/c.php?g=777192&p=5574741.

University of Michigan LSA Learning & Teaching Consultants (n.d.). Infographic assignments: Blending creative and critical. https://lsa.umich.edu/technology-services/news-events/all-news/teaching-tip-of-the-week/infographic-assignments–blending-creative-and-critical.html.

Varsavsky, C., & Rayner, G. (2013). Strategies that challenge: Exploring the use of differentiated assessment to challenge high-achieving students in large enrollment undergraduate cohorts. *Assessment and Evaluation in Higher Education*, 38(7), 789–802.

Wasson, B. (1996). Instructional planning and contemporary theories of learning: Is this a self-contradiction? In P. Brna, A. Paiva, & J. Self (Eds.), *Proceedings of the European Conference on Artificial Intelligence in Education* (pp. 23–30). Colibri.

Wollschleger, J. (2019). Making it count: Using real-world projects for course assignments. *Teaching Sociology*, 47(4), 314–324.

Wright, N. D., & Larsen, V. (2016). Improving marketing students' writing skills using a one-page paper. *Marketing Education Review*, 26(1), 25–32. doi:10.1080/10528008.2015.1091666.

Wu, K. (2020, November 2). Scientific journals commit to diversity but lack the data. *New York Times*. https://www.nytimes.com/2020/10/30/science/diversity-science-journals.html#:~:text=Several%20prominent%20publishers%20said%20they,researchers%20contributing%20to%20their%20platforms.&text=Sign%20up%20for%20Science%20Times,cosmos%20and%20the%20human%20body.

Yosso, T. J. (2005). Whose culture has capital? A critical race theory discussion of community cultural wealth. *Race, Ethnicity, & Education*, 8(1), 69–91. https://doi.org/10.1080/1361332052000341006.

Zakrajsek, T. (2022). *The new science of learning* (3rd ed.). Routledge.

Chapter 6

Giving Choice in Assignments

Myra J. George and Jennifer E. Thompson

It was 3:45 pm, and Jana, a sociology professor at a local college, had just spent the last 15 minutes enthusiastically introducing the next assignment: a five-generation family-tree project that involved research. This was one of Jana's favorite assignments, and she had included it in her course for several years. The students were mostly silent, attempting to process the information. Cynthia, an African American student, wondered how she would be able to trace her family back five generations given the history of record-keeping for Black families and the absence of reliable, comprehensive databases. Michael wondered how he could trace his family history given that his mother was adopted. And Larry was trying to decide how he would handle his parents' same-sex marriage—a topic he did not typically discuss with his classmates. On the face of it, Jana's assignment seemed fine, but upon reflection on the cultural diversity in the course, it created the potential for student anxiety, decreased motivation, and disengagement.

Jana's approach to the assignment is not unique. In many traditional courses, all facets of learning have been pre-established before the students arrive at the virtual or physical door. In most cases, the instructor has developed the policies and procedures for the course and packaged them into a syllabus that is reviewed in the first week of classes. The assignments have been created, and there are often very specific guidelines that offer little flexibility. In such settings, students are expected to learn and demonstrate competency in the same ways. Consequently, they typically do not have much of an opportunity to bring their own experiences into the learning environment and, depending on how the assignments and course structure have been designed, they may or may not be able to connect their experiences to those of their classmates or build relationships with other students.

While pre-planning is both necessary and expected, an inflexible plan can create barriers to success for students. Considering the hypothetical experiences of Cynthia, Michael, and Larry, the glaring lesson for educators is that a "one-size-fits-all" approach falls short of an effective

DOI: 10.4324/9781003443797-7

teaching model. Indeed, in a 2023 Student Voice survey conducted by *Inside Higher Ed*, over 3,000 college students were asked to describe strategies professors could use to help them be more successful, and the top three responses were related to flexibility and variety (Flaherty, 2023). Students felt they would be more successful academically if instructors were more flexible with deadlines (57 percent), varied their teaching styles (51 percent), and were less rigid with regard to attendance and participation. Teaching can be more effective when both content and instructional methods evolve with the changing times and accommodate learners' differences.

Ideally, educators want all students to feel seen and valued in their courses, yet Jana's assignment did not seem to consider the various backgrounds of the students on her course. It may be impossible for an instructor to plan for every kind of cultural background, especially because often important cultural markers may be invisible, but giving students choices about their assignments is one way to acknowledge and affirm their cultures. Moreover, this approach allows students to craft products that are meaningful and relevant, and it may reduce their anxiety.

This chapter explores the research related to student learning autonomy and suggests practical ways in which instructors can enable students to exercise choice in their assignments—a culturally affirming strategy.

Why Choice Matters

Motivation theories suggest that a simple way to combat anxiety and low levels of engagement and motivation associated with the "one-size-fits-all" approach is to give students options or choices. One widely known motivational theory is self-determination theory (Deci & Ryan, 1985), which focuses on three basic and interconnected human needs: autonomy, competency, and relatedness. When applied to learning, self-determination theory suggests that students are motivated to perform well when they feel they have some control over what and how they will learn, such as by bringing their own experiences into the learning process (autonomy); believe they are capable of completing the learning tasks (competence); and have a sense that their experiences are reflected in the learning process and that they have been allowed to affiliate with their classmates (relatedness). Self-determination "involves the experience of choice. [It is] the capacity to choose and have those choices ... be the determinants of one's actions" (Deci & Ryan, 1985, p. 38). Deci and Ryan (1985) believed that choice-rich learning environments help foster all three of these motivating factors.

Additionally, offering choice shifts the typical power dynamic of the classroom. In a limited-choice environment, the instructor makes most of the decisions about what will be taught and the type of work the students will do, but students can feel more empowered when they are given the opportunity to participate in the decision-making. Having a role in making decisions about learning processes, including assignments, can be motivational for all students, but especially for students who may have felt excluded or marginalized previously. Instructors can create opportunities for students to be autonomous learners to increase student motivation and engagement (Vansteenkiste et al., 2004).

Choices are also an excellent way for students to pursue learning activities that are aligned with their interests and goals. According to the expectancy-value model (Eccles & Wigfield, 1995), students are more likely to be motivated when they expect to be successful in tasks that they value. Eccles and Wigfield (1995) identified three types of value: attainment value (importance); intrinsic value (the pleasure derived from the task); and utility value (its usefulness in achieving a short- or long-term goal). Arend and Carlson (Chapter 3) discuss the importance of assignments connecting to current and future goals. When a task challenges students in ways that support their personal and professional short- and long-term goals, they are likely to exert more effort and persist for longer because they see the assignment as an investment in their development (Hulleman et al., 2016). Unsurprisingly, the increased effort and persistence often lead to higher levels of achievement (Eccles and Wigfield, 1995). Students will likely display increased motivation and a greater desire to complete the assignment when they are permitted to choose the learning task (Peláez Galán, 2016).

Patall et al. (2008, p. 270) conducted a meta-analysis of 41 studies on student choice and concluded that "providing choice enhanced intrinsic motivation, effort, task performance, and perceived competence, among other outcomes." Other researchers have found that choice is associated with increased pleasure during the learning process and perceived competence (Birdsell et al., 2009). The latter benefit is especially important because confident students are more likely to seek out additional learning opportunities that will enable them to develop their skills. Moreover, research has shown that it is helpful to provide students with topic choices that interest them as this fosters a sense of ownership (Birdsell et al., 2009). A study of students in a physical science course Milner-Bolotin (2001) found that those who chose a project topic based on their interests experienced improved learning. Providing choice in assignments also enables students to acquire and develop skill sets that they can apply beyond the course (Anderson, 2016).

Furthermore, facilitating choice often generates healthier energy among students. It can reduce competition in the classroom because students may not have to worry as much about being compared to their peers. Grading systems are typically either norm-referenced (students are evaluated in comparison to one another) or criterion-referenced (students are evaluated using a set of criteria). Often, in courses with little or no choice, students believe that the instructor will use norm-referenced grading. By contrast, in courses that are choice-rich, students feel that instructors are more likely to use criterion-referenced grading. Thus, allowing students to make choices allows them to focus on leveraging their performance and mitigates anxiety that their peers might outperform them. In turn, this can lead to more effective collaboration, as students tend to be more supportive of their classmates if they feel they are not in competition with them. Choice can also generate pleasure and positivity. When students have "some power and control" over their learning choices, they are more likely to enjoy the work (Anderson, 2016, p. 20).

Admittedly, designing a choice-rich learning environment places certain demands on the instructor, but the benefits of adopting this approach can be considerable. For example, instructors who allow students to choose their topics may discover that they expand their knowledge base and cultural competence. It would be virtually impossible for a single instructor to imagine all the possible topics related to a concept or all the authors and poets who have written on a subject. Thus, when a creative writing instructor asks their students to write a children's story about a cultural holiday, they may learn about Ramadan, sitting up with the dead, when a baby should get their first haircut, making tamales, not buying a headstone until a year of grieving has passed, or countless other possibilities.

Relatedly, allowing students to choose can break up the monotony that instructors sometimes feel when they teach the same courses term after term or grade numerous assignments where all students had to follow the same requirements. An instructor who allows students to choose the topic and the assignment product never knows precisely what to expect, so the teaching experience is fresh each time. As students submit their assignment products, the instructor has new exemplars to add to the course.

Finally, course planning for choice and equitable outcomes may foster continuous quality improvement as instructors reflect on what went well with the choices offered, what could be improved, and what they could do differently in the future. Essentially, choice in assignments makes for a better learning environment for students and educators alike.

Choice and Learning Outcomes

Learning outcomes drive all course design decisions (see Chapter 1), so it is important for instructors who are considering how to make their courses more choice-rich to develop assignments that align with the learning outcomes. They need to ask themselves: "What students should know or be able to do by the end of this course, and how does each specific assignment provide them with an opportunity to demonstrate that they have acquired this knowledge or developed this ability?"

Determining appropriate assignment choices can require a learning curve and takes practice to develop. Anchoring assignments, especially ones that are culturally affirming and meaningful, to the learning outcomes is critical and requires significant cognitive effort and time; however, this front-end investment will be worthwhile. Students will undoubtedly appreciate the infusion of choice into the course and will be more likely to find assignments culturally affirming and meaningful (see Chapter 2).

Not all choices are created equal, however. Instructors must ensure that all options provide evidence of the same learning outcomes. For example, if a learning outcome is for students to find and critically evaluate sources of information, each assignment option needs to provide a path for students to develop and showcase this skill. A traditional research paper could be one type of product, but Winfield (Chapter 5) challenges instructors to think beyond traditional assignments and identify more creative options. For example, a podcast, Padlet (digital bulletin board), or infographic might allow students to demonstrate their competency in evaluating sources. On the other hand, an original poem may not be the best way for this outcome to be demonstrated, because outside sources are not typically consulted or evaluated when writing verse.

One tactic an instructor can use to determine if different assignment options are equitable is to consider each one carefully in terms of learning, skills, and effort. Arend and Carlson (Chapter 3) suggest listing the skills that will be learned during each assignment. Skills connected to the learning outcome will likely be the same for various options, but different assignments may help students develop different transferable skills, such as presentation or technology skills. Instructors can reflect on how strongly each assignment connects to the identified course learning outcomes and identify the skills students will develop by working on the different assignment options. Instructors could also estimate the amount of time each activity will take to complete. It can be helpful to request input from colleagues and students during this process. Assignments may then be modified to ensure they are similar in terms of time investment and learning. Students could also be asked to report the amount of time they spent on the various assignment tasks. Engaging in this reflective process can help instructors determine if modifications to assignment options are needed.

Some Words of Caution

Sometimes choices are too complex, too numerous, or too similar, all of which can hinder rather than enhance the learning experience. According to Iyengar and Lepper (2000, p. 996), people "have difficulty managing complex choices" or navigating choice overload. When faced with complex choices, they are likely to employ a process of elimination or resort to selecting what they believe to be the safest choice. Similarly, when given too many options, regardless of their complexity, students may choose randomly, give up their right to choose, or allow someone to choose for them, all of which can potentially undermine the universal need for competence (Parker et al., 2017).

Altogether, the various forms of choice overload create more rules for decision-making, to the detriment of the enjoyability and cognitive stimulus that choice is meant to bring. This can lead to superficial or disingenuous processes such as heuristics that involve taking shortcuts to reach an easy or fast decision (Cherry, 2022). As a result, offering choices in these cases is counterproductive, as students are likely to experience dissatisfaction and demotivation.

This overload risk can be mitigated by limiting the number of choices students are given. It can be helpful for instructors to give students a list of options. Sometimes just two will be enough to foster autonomy and increase motivation, but instructors could add a third where a student can present an idea for an alternative product or approach for instructor approval. This combined approach of presenting a small number of options plus an "other" option can work well because it provides structure to those who need it but also flexibility and freedom to those who prefer to exercise more control over their learning journey.

Moreover, offering choices in assignment products may not always be feasible in classes such as nursing and teacher education, where students are expected to complete an external assessment in a specific format. If students in an electrical lineman program must take a pole-climbing exam to gain an apprenticeship, offering options for them to take quizzes, create posters, or write essays may not prepare them for the final assessment. Such students would be better served by assignments that involve climbing poles.

Lastly, for text-based assignments, giving students unfettered autonomy to choose their topics has the potential to increase the risk of infractions related to academic integrity. Students who are in the early stages of higher education may not yet have discovered their interests. If pressed for time or unable to brainstorm effectively, they may be tempted to choose a topic that allows them to download a product easily from the Internet or use an artificial intelligence tool. Theoretically, allowing students to choose their topics may increase their sense of ownership, thereby reducing the likelihood of plagiarism or reliance on AI tools, but it is important for instructors to consider ways to reduce the temptation for students to seek out these tools.

Types of Choice

Dabrowski and Marshall (2018) described three types of choice: content, product, and process. Content choices allow students to determine the topics of and learning resources for their assignments; product choices enable students to select how they will demonstrate their learning; and process choices give students ownership over decisions about who to work with on projects or due dates for assignments.

Content Choices

One of the most common ways in which instructors offer choice is by allowing students to choose the assignment topic or the resources they may use within it. This approach can be empowering, motivating, and culturally affirming because it allows students to choose texts or topics that they find interesting, relevant, and meaningful. A student who feels demotivated by the prospect of writing about the poetry of Emily Dickinson or the short stories of Edgar Allan Poe might be excited to analyze the poetry of Joy Harjo or the short stories of Isabel Allende.

Instructors have used three primary approaches to give students content choices: first, an unrestricted, open-ended choice, whereby students are allowed to choose any topic as long as it is related to the course; second, a guided choice, through which students choose from within parameters that the instructor has established; and, third, a hybrid choice, where instructors provide a list of at least two options but also allow students to make their own suggestions.

Open-Ended Topic Choice

A significant advantage of giving students open-ended choice is that it allows the students to make selections that affirm their culture(s), as opposed to the instructor trying to identify potentially affirming options on the basis of assumptions. Even the most highly trained instructor cannot maintain expertise in every possible cultural group. Moreover, cultural nuances require effective and sensitive navigation. Giving students full freedom to choose a topic shifts autonomy to them and enables them to choose a culturally relevant topic. For instance, a rural student may decide that they do not want to do yet another project about farm life.

Guided Topic Choice

Guided choices can be useful because students can find open-ended decision-making time-consuming or overwhelming, whereas they may be inspired by examples. When using a guided approach, instructors provide a list of topics from which students can choose, rather than giving them complete freedom to select any subject. For example, an English instructor might ask students to write a literary analysis essay that focuses on an element of literature of their choosing, such as characterization, but provide a list of acceptable texts. Another example would be an instructor who asks students to write about environmental injustice within their communities but allows them to decide what form of environmental injustice they want to research.

Instructors who use a guided approach might provide an umbrella-like topic that will allow students to personalize the broader topic in culturally meaningful ways. For example, an economics or business instructor who wants students to explore reparations might allow them to explore the impact of this policy on Native Americans, Japanese Americans, ADOS (American descendants of slaves), or another group of their choosing. All students will learn about the same policy, but in a manner that is tailored to their individual interests.

Instructors might decide to use a guided-choice approach to ensure that they are familiar with the text under discussion. Generally speaking, an instructor needs to be well acquainted with the foundational text in order to assess the accuracy and thoroughness of a student's discussion or analysis. Clearly, then, if students were given complete freedom to choose any topic or text, the instructor would be obliged to invest significant time and effort in reading or viewing all the selected sources before grading the assignments. Providing a limited but diverse set of options is often a good solution because it limits the burden on the instructor while still giving students some ownership and autonomy over their learning. For example, rather than letting a class of 20 students study any topic they wish, the instructor might allow each student to choose from a list of just five options.

Ensuring Options Are Culturally Affirming

Regardless of the breadth of choice an instructor elects to provide, they should consider whether they are giving students culturally affirming choices. Instructors need to determine if topic options represent issues that are relevant to students of various genders, races, ages, and other characteristics. For instance, a biology or nursing instructor who wants students to complete poster presentations on diseases should ensure the options are inclusive and relevant to every member of the class, regardless of race, gender, or age. Consequently, the list of options might include sickle cell anemia, osteoporosis, Gaucher disease, and others. Similarly, an economics instructor who wants students to explore market collapses might include Tulsa's Black Wall Street as an option.

While instructors may be able to brainstorm choices that consider culture, it is also important for them to keep in mind the concept of affirmation. Ideally, topics should represent positive, or at least balanced, aspects of culture. In other words, the history instructor who offers just two options—African American slavery and Mexican farm workers—for an essay assignment may not affirm the full range of the cultural experience. By contrast, the hybrid approach, which involves providing students with diverse yet specific topic options while also allowing them to choose a topic that is not on the instructor's list, or tailor the list to their own cultural experiences, can be empowering and supportive.

Source Choice

Another form of content choice is allowing students to choose their own sources, such as books, articles, videos, podcasts, and so forth, rather than requiring them to consult only those selected by the instructor. Brian Kayser involved students in the process of determining culturally affirming resources by encouraging them to identify and evaluate books using a diversity lens (see Appendix, Example 20).

Variety and flexibility are key. The commuter student who spends 35 minutes in her car driving home every Wednesday evening might wish to listen to an audio recording of a chapter or a podcast rather than read the content in book form. Similarly, providing links to videos can support student success by allowing them to pause and rewind as they grapple with challenging concepts.

Product Choice

In addition to adopting an approach that gives students more choice over course content, topics, and resources, instructors might consider giving them more freedom to choose assignment products. Students are rarely given options in relation to how they demonstrate their learning, with many instructors continuing to rely on traditional assessments such as exams and research papers, though there is some evidence that this is starting to change (see Harrington, 2023). Winfield (Chapter 5) highlights the challenges of these traditional assessments and encourages instructors to consider different options. Giving students more creative ways to demonstrate their learning and letting them choose from a list of assignment methods can be motivating (Patall et al., 2008).

More often than not, there is more than one way that students can demonstrate their mastery of course concepts (see Chapter 3). For example, they could be encouraged to demonstrate their learning and creativity through skits, podcasts, websites, TED talks, welding products, or multimedia essays. Consider the sociology instructor who wants students to learn how to summarize sources and construct an annotated bibliography of texts on the same general topic. Students who create an annotated Spotify music playlist can demonstrate the same proficiency in extracting key ideas and critically evaluating concepts as those who write a traditional bibliography, and they may find the task much more relevant and satisfying. At Winston-Salem State University, education course students were given a list of assignment options, including writing a poem, writing a story, drawing a series of illustrations, creating a short graphic novel, or writing lyrics to a song/rap to demonstrate what they had learned from reading an assigned text (Dreyfus et al., 2023). At the same institution, a math instructor offered a variety of options, including taking a traditional cumulative final exam, creating a music video, preparing a graphic project, and constructing a reference sheet (Dreyfus et al., 2023). Creating assignment products that leave room for innovation and allow students to select options that enable them to build on their strengths and develop the skills they need to achieve their goals can be very motivating.

There is also evidence that providing students with assignment product options can result in a more equitable learning path. Research has shown that performance assessments can vary based on assignment type. For example, Singer-Freeman et al. (2019) found that multiple-choice exam questions often led to grades that did not reflect student competence in the subject matter due to their reliance on sophisticated sentence structures. Likewise, other studies have suggested that formal essays and research papers can lead to disparities. Applying a culturally relevant theoretical matrix, Hobbs and Robinson (2022) studied assignment types in courses at a liberal arts college, a community college, and a large urban research university. Their analysis identified educational equity gaps across all three institutions when students were assessed through formal essays or research papers that had low inclusive content and low utility value.

One way to incorporate product assignment choice is the menu approach, which has been widely used with contract grading. Although there are many variations of this approach, Volk (2016) identified three common forms: negotiated, non-negotiated, and community-based contracts. Fundamentally, in contract grading, students are presented with an array of assignment products, each with a point value. Each student then selects the products they wish to complete and, by extension, the grade they hope to achieve. So, for example, the instructor might create a grading scale in which students must earn at least 90 points to attain an A. Then, at the start of the course, the instructor distributes a list of assignments and their point values. For example, a one-page chapter summary might be worth 10 points, a research paper 50 points, an oral presentation 40 points, and so on. The point values will typically reflect the relative complexity of the assignments (i.e., length, presumed time for completion) as well as the number of learning outcomes addressed by each product.

In a negotiated system, each student chooses assignments from the instructor's list to correspond with the course grade they wish to achieve. In other words, a student who wants an A grade will select more assignments (or more complex assignments) than a student who is content with a C grade. The instructor will meet with every student to discuss their choices and expectations, which may result in revisions to the proposed contract. In essence, then, the final contract is co-constructed. By contrast, in a non-negotiated contract, students choose their assignments with minimal, if any, input from the instructor. In both approaches, each student prepares and signs a formal contract listing their chosen assignments, and their final grade is based on the contract and their performance. In the community-based contract grading approach, the entire class chooses assignments from the instructor's menu, rather than each individual student making their own selection. According to Moreno-Lopez (2005), negotiated contracts support learner autonomy through shared decision-making.

Certainly, allowing students to choose their academic products can be time-consuming for faculty. This is especially true for new instructors and instructors who are teaching a new course. Identifying multiple types of products that equitably address learning outcomes and offer culturally affirming and meaningful ways for students to engage in and demonstrate their learning invariably takes time and effort (see Chapter 1). Fortunately, though, instructors have access to some helpful resources. First, they can reach out to colleagues in their own and other institutions for information about the various types of assignments. In addition, they can tap into discipline-specific learning communities through professional organizations to gain further insights and inspiration. Finally, some college, university, and organizational websites offer examples that can be useful for instructors who are striving to identify creative assignment product options.

Process Choice

Another strategy for giving students greater autonomy is process choice. This includes allowing students to decide when their work needs to be submitted and whether assignments should be completed independently or in a group. Research has shown that process choice is rarely offered to students (Harrington, 2023), yet it is a great way to help them develop ownership over their learning experience.

With regard to due dates, either the whole class could determine the submission date for a particular assignment, or the instructor may opt to allow each student to determine their own deadline. Instructors can establish parameters for these decisions. For example, the class might be given the option of Sunday or Monday evenings for weekly online discussions, or before or after spring break for submission of a major project.

On the surface, allowing each student to set their own due dates might be viewed as especially challenging, but once again setting parameters can make the process more manageable. For example, if students are given the option of submitting an assignment before or after spring break, the instructor could specify two due dates. This could be a great way to distribute grading work over two weeks rather than one, while also giving the students a degree of process choice.

Process choices can also be applied to how students work together. For example, students engaging in group projects may be allowed to choose the composition of each group among themselves. Similarly, instructors can create roles within the groups and then let the members decide which student is best suited to each role. For example, Myers (2023) suggests that a small group discussion about a literary text might include a researcher (who will find and summarize a related article), a multimedia director (who will find a video or audio clip related to the reading), a rewriter (who will rewrite a scene using a different voice), a historian (who will track the major events and create a timeline), and a discussion director (who will prepare discussion questions for the group).

Allowing students to choose how they interact and engage with each other is consistent with universal design for learning principles. Moreover, this strategy has been found to support learners with disabilities and social phobias (Sacco et al., 2020). It is important to note, however, that if students are given complete freedom to choose their group members, the resulting groups may be more homogeneous, which may hinder attainment of the highest levels of learning (Hinds et al., 2000). In addition, a self-selection approach could be detrimental to students of color and students with lower ability levels (Shimazoe & Aldrich, 2010). Thus, caution is needed when determining how much latitude students are allowed.

Students can also be given the option of working independently or with a partner or small group. Those who have demanding schedules that make meeting with group members difficult may appreciate the option of working independently. Meanwhile, others may prioritize the support they receive when working as part of a group. One concern is that students who opt out of group work may not develop essential collaboration and teamwork skills. To combat this potential problem, students could be given this option for only one or two assignments over the duration of the course.

Conclusion

Research has shown that giving students greater choice over their assignments is associated with increased motivation and learning. As instructors consider the various options for assignments, it is important to ensure that they are aligned with the course learning outcomes and reflect the students' diverse cultures and lived experiences. There are three main types of assignment choices: content, product, and process. Instructors can allow students to choose topics or resources, how they will demonstrate their learning, and even when their assignments are due and with whom they will work. However, guided choices, which offer a limited number of options, may be more practical than giving students free rein. Allowing them to choose between just two options can increase student ownership of the learning experience and can be culturally affirming and meaningful.

Reflection Questions

1 What type of choices are you most inclined to offer students? Why?
2 What choices do students have in terms of assignment content in your courses? Which cultures are represented, and in what way, in topic and source choices?
3 What product choices are offered to students? How can you ensure that various product options require similar amounts of effort and learning, and that they are aligned with course learning outcomes?
4 What types of process choices are you building into your courses?
5 What are the benefits of guided choices, and how can you apply guided choices to your course design and delivery?
6 How does incorporating choice impact your workload, and what could you do to make your workload more manageable while still offering choice?

References

Anderson, M. (2016). *Learning to choose, choosing to learn: The key to student motivation and achievement*. Association for Supervision & Curriculum Development.
Birdsell, B. S., Ream, S. M., Seyller, A. M., & Zobott, P. L. (2009). Motivating students by increasing student choice. Master's thesis, Saint Xavier University. https://files.eric.ed.gov/fulltext/ED504816.pdf.
Cherry, K. (2022, November 8). What are heuristics? These mental shortcuts can help people make decisions more efficiently. Very Well Mind. https://www.verywellmind.com/what-is-a-heuristic-2795235.
Dabrowski, J., & Marshall, T. R. (2018, November). Motivation and engagement in student assignments: The role of choice and relevancy. The Education Trust. https://edtrust.org/resource/motivation-and-engagement-in-student-assignments/.
Deci, E. L., and Ryan, R. M. (1985). *Intrinsic motivation and self-determination in human behavior*. Plenum.
Dreyfus, K. S., Bradley, S., Crist, L., & Thomas, C. (2023). *Case studies for assessing students in equitable ways*. UNC Assessment and Accreditation Council.
Eccles, J. S., & Wigfield, A. (1995). In the mind of the actor: The structure of adolescents' achievement task values and expectancy-related beliefs. *Personality and Social Psychology Bulletin*, 21(3), 215–225. doi:10.1177/0146167295213003.
Flaherty, C. (2023, March 23). What students want (and don't) from their professors. *Inside Higher Ed*. https://www.insidehighered.com/news/2023/03/24/survey-faculty-teaching-style-impedes-academic-success-students-say.
Harrington, C. (2023). How much have psychology assignments changed over time? A descriptive study. *Journal for Research and Practice in College Teaching*, 8(1), 1–14. https://journals.uc.edu/index.php/jrpct/issue/view/521.
Hinds, P. J., Carley, K. M., Krackhardt, D., & Wholey, D. (2000). Choosing work group members: Balancing similarity, competence, and familiarity. *Organizational Behavior and Human Decision Processes*, 81(2), 226–251. doi:10.1006/obhd.1999.2875.

Hobbs, H., & Robinson, C. (2022). Culturally relevant assessment. In G. W. Henning, G. R. Baker, N. A. Jankowski, A. E. Lundquist, & E. Montenegro (Eds.), *Reframing assessment to center equity: Theories, models, and practices* (pp. 145–165). Routledge.

Hulleman, C. S., Barron, K. E., Kosovich, J. J., & Lazowski, R. A. (2016). Student motivation: Current theories, constructs, and interventions within an expectancy-value framework. In A. A. Lipnevich, F. Preckel, & R. D. Roberts (Eds.), *Psychosocial skills and school systems in the 21st century: Theory, research, and practice* (pp. 241–278). Springer International Publishing.

Iyengar, S., & Lepper, M. (2000). When choice is demotivating: Can one desire too much of a good thing? *Journal of Personality and Social Psychology*, 79(6), 995–1006. doi:10.1037//0022-3514.79.6.995.

Milner-Bolotin, M. (2001). The effects of topic choice in project-based instruction on undergraduate physical science students' interest, ownership, and motivation. Doctoral dissertation, University of Texas at Austin. https://www.proquest.com/dissertations-theses/effects-topic-choice-project-based-instruction-on/docview/304720967/se-2.

Moreno-Lopez, I. (2005). Sharing power with students: The critical language classroom. *Radical Pedagogy*, 7(2). https://radicalpedagogy.icaap.org/content/issue7_2/moreno.html.

Myers, A. (2023, June 6). Personal communication.

Parker, F., Novak, J., & Bartell, T. (2017). To engage students, give them meaningful choices in the classroom. *Phi Delta Kappa*, 99(2), 37–41.

Patall, E. A., Cooper, H., & Robinson, J. C. (2008). The effects of choice on intrinsic motivation and related outcomes: A meta-analysis of research findings. *Psychological Bulletin*, 134(2), 270–300.

Peláez Galán, P. (2016). The effect of multimodality in increasing motivation and collaboration among 4th CSE EFL learners: A case study. https://www.academia.edu/29341844/The_Effect_of_Multimodality_in_Increasing_Motivation_and_Collaboration_among_4th_CSE_EFL_Students.

Sacco, D., Redmond, R., & Latulipe, C. (2020). Addressing access in active learning. In J. A. Keith & M. P. Morgan (Eds.), *Faculty experiences in active learning: A collection of strategies for implementing active learning across disciplines* (pp. 73–85). J. Murrey Atkins Library at UNC Charlotte. https://doi.org/10.5149/9781469660042_Keith-Le.

Shimazoe, J., & Aldrich, H. (2010). Group work can be gratifying: Understanding and overcoming resistance to cooperative learning. *College Teaching*, 58(2), 52–57. doi:10.1080/87567550903418594.

Singer-Freeman, K. E., Hobbs, H., & Robinson, C. (2019). Theoretical matrix of culturally relevant assessment. *Assessment Update*, 31(4), 1–2.

Vansteenkiste, M. et al. (2004). Motivating learning, performance, and persistence: The synergistic effects of intrinsic goal contents and autonomy-supportive contexts. *Journal of Personality and Social Psychology*, 87(2), 246–260. doi:10.1037/0022-3514.87.2.246.

Volk, S. (2016, March 27). Contract improv: Three approaches to contract grading. *After Class: Education & Democracy*. https://steven-volk.blog/2016/03/27/contract-improv-three-approaches-to-contract-grading/.

Chapter 7

Being Transparent about Assignment Expectations

Ellen Wasserman and Tadé Ayeni

Alexia was almost in tears. She had come to the college writing tutoring center desperate to find a way to improve her grade in English 101. For the two essays she had written so far, she had received an F and a D. There were only two further essay assignments in the course, and she knew she was in danger of failing. "I just don't understand it," she moaned. "I always got As in high school. I thought for sure this class would be easy for me. I thought I was a decent writer, but now I feel like I have no idea what I'm doing!"

A few tissues later, Alexia and her tutor looked at the next essay assignment, a research paper about a topic of her choice. As they read through it, the tutor started to see the problem. The direction on the assignment sheet focused on formatting details, grammar mistakes to avoid, and websites that should not be used for the research, but there was no information on the purpose of the assignment and little guidance on how to approach it. No wonder Alexia felt that she did not know what she was doing or why she was even doing the assignment in the first place.

Alexia and the tutor formulated a list of specific questions for the instructor. Alexia then headed off to the computer lab to write an email to her instructor, asking for more direction. She agreed to come back to the tutor the following week with the instructor's response and an outline of the paper. After Alexia left the room, the tutor took a moment to vow that she would always follow transparency guidelines in her classes so her students would know why they were doing each assignment, what they needed to do to complete it successfully, and how their work would be evaluated.

Why Transparent Assignments Matter

The Transparency in Learning and Teaching (TILT) framework—a process for creating transparent activities and assignments that improve learning for all students—was developed to support underserved, first-year college students and thereby have a positive impact on retention (Winkelmes et al.,

DOI: 10.4324/9781003443797-8

2016). Transparent assignments include a purpose, a list of steps or tasks, and assessment criteria that can lead to deeper learning and more equitable outcomes (Winkelmes, 2013). Both students and instructors benefit when assignment expectations are communicated in a transparent way.

Student Benefits

Transparent assignments pave the way for student success. Students have reported feeling more confident and less stressed when presented with transparent assignments (Anderson et al., 2013; Angel & Merken, 2021; Peplow et al., 2021). Winkelmes et al. (2015) also reported that when an assignment contains a clear description of the purpose, tasks, and criteria, students often have higher levels of confidence, self-efficacy, and motivation. In a study of seven minority-serving institutions that focused on exploring teaching practices designed to support underserved first-year college students, Winkelmes et al. (2016) found that transparent assignments increased students' sense of belonging, improved academic confidence, had a positive impact on the quality of work, and reduced questions and confusion. Students who were given transparent assignments also increased their mastery of specific skills valued by future employers. For example, they learned how to make connections between a variety of sources, apply skills to a variety of contexts, write more clearly, evaluate the reliability of information from various sources, and consider others' opinions and points of view.

In their guide to inclusive teaching, Sathy and Hogan (n.d.) noted that providing more structure and transparency is beneficial for all students; conversely, when structure and transparency are lacking, many students are negatively impacted and put at an academic disadvantage. Transparent assignments are especially beneficial for students in their first year of college as they attempt to familiarize themselves with the expectations of their new learning environment (Leuzinger & Grallo, 2019; Peplow et al., 2021). They may also be beneficial for members of historically marginalized populations, including first-generation, low-income, and underserved students.

Transparent assignments take the guesswork out of courses by helping students navigate the "hidden curriculum" of college expectations and illuminating the learning skills and behaviors they need to be successful (Peplow et al., 2021). According to Peplow et al. (2021), traditional learning models that rely on students' understanding of college expectations can arbitrarily disadvantage and isolate those who do not possess this knowledge. By contrast, transparent assignments eliminate the invisible prerequisites that put some learners at a disadvantage. For example, if an assignment asks the class to find and evaluate research, a student who understands what is meant by "research" and "evaluation" will know how to approach the task successfully. Conversely, if a student does not know what the instructor means by "research" and "evaluation," they may approach the task in a way that does not meet the instructor's expectations. Both students may invest similar levels of effort and time, but the student who can infer the instructor's expectations will likely perform better than the one who does not fully understand the terminology. When instructors use concise, unambiguous language, explain all terms, and avoid acronyms, the overall purpose of the assignment and component tasks are clearer for all students, regardless of their college knowledge. This can be especially helpful to first-generation students who may not have a family member who can provide advice.

Key barriers to equity in the classroom are the unstated expectations of college both within and outside the classroom. Although unstated, these expectations will likely be readily apparent to students with family and friends who have been to college, and those who attended high schools that do a good job of preparing their students for college. By contrast, first-generation students, and those who attended underfunded high schools, may find it extremely difficult to decipher unstated expectations because no one in their informal networks will have any knowledge of them. Transparent assignments can help to resolve this disparity.

> While it has a positive effect for all students, the effect is more significant for students who are non-White, first-generation students, and non-traditional students. Transparent design also helps mitigate some executive function challenges, like difficulty getting started, feeling overwhelmed, and having trouble making connections between an assignment and the "big picture" of a course or program.
> (Toy, 2022)

Instructor Benefits

Instructors can also reap rich benefits from adopting transparent assignments, including thinking more deeply about their expectations and goals. For example, in a study at the University of Nevada Las Vegas, an associate professor who teaches introductory science courses asserted: "This has not only changed how I approach each assignment but also each class meeting. Incorporating the purpose/task/criteria framework helps me focus on the main goals for each day, which helps students see the purpose of every class session" (Winkelmes et al., 2015, p. 5). Using transparent assignment design also helps instructors align class activities and assignments with learning outcomes and assessments (Fisher et al., 2016).

Students are more likely to meet their instructors' expectations when they are given transparent assignments. As a result, instructors have found "the number of questions (especially frantic, last-minute ones) about assignments has decreased, and those that remain are usually thoughtful questions that lead to useful conversations" (Winkelmes et al., 2015, p. 5).

Table 7.1 provides an overview of the benefits of transparent assignments for both students and instructors.

What Are Transparent Assignments?

Transparent assignments aim to provide clear instructions to students on why the assignment is required, what they need to do to complete it, and how they will be graded on their work. According to Winkelmes's (2013) TILT framework, this translates into three main transparent assignment principles: purpose, tasks, and criteria for success. Students will better understand the assignment and know how best to approach it when all three of these principles are clearly stated. For example, in a community portrait assignment, Brie Morettini provided students with a clear overview of the constituent parts of the assignment and explained how these were related (see Appendix, Example 19).

Purpose

According to the TILT framework, a purpose statement gives the instructor an opportunity to clarify the content and skills students will learn during the assignment and explain how the task relates to the course learning outcomes (Winkelmes et al., 2015). Morales and Olivares-Urueta (Chapter 1) emphasize the importance of considering course learning outcomes when designing courses and communicating this to students.

Explaining the immediate and future value of the assignment can help students understand why it is an important learning activity (see Chapter 3). The assignment's purpose may relate to students' academic and career

Table 7.1 Benefits of Transparent Assignments

Students	Instructors
• Builds confidence and self-efficacy • Increases motivation • Improves academic performance • Increases mastery of skills found most valuable by employers • Increases critical thinking and quality of work • Increases engagement • Increases familiarity with expectations, actions to complete tasks, and grading schemes	• Provides new insights into how to structure assignments and goals for class sessions • Improves alignment of class activities with assignments, learning outcomes, and assessments • Results in fewer questions about assignments • Increases the quality of student work and reduces grading time

goals and can create a context for developing knowledge and skills. Students are more likely to engage in activities and assignments when they know why they will be practicing a certain technique or deepening their understanding of a particular concept (Angel & Merken, 2021). The TILT framework advises instructors to explain not just the skills the students will acquire but also how they will be able to employ those skills throughout the course, in future courses, in their field of study, and in their professional lives beyond college (Winkelmes, 2013). Instructors can make this explanation readily accessible to students by presenting it in a class session and including it in the syllabus and the assignment description (Angel & Merken, 2021).

Every purpose statement should explain the reasons for the task and what the students will get out of doing it (Bhavsar, 2020). For example, Bhavsar (2020) found it useful to provide a detailed explanation of the purpose of pre-reading and submitting notes on the readings as a graded assignment. From this purpose statement, students learned that preview reading would increase their understanding of complex content and so make it easier for them to participate in classroom discussions and activities. In addition, the statement explained that the assignment would help them learn new information, develop and practice key academic skills, and enhance their memories by encouraging them to make connections. As a result, students did "80–90% of the assigned reading in a content-heavy, flipped science course" (Bhavsar, 2020, p. 34).

Several researchers have found that discussing the learning goals of an assignment and the rationale behind the design enhances student engagement and learning (Anderson et al., 2013; Winkelmes, 2013; Winkelmes et al., 2015). Students respond positively to learning about the purpose of assignments and activities and report that acquiring this knowledge helps them think more critically about the content (Anderson et al., 2013). Understanding an assignment's purpose not only helped students prepare mentally for it but also increased their appreciation of their learning experience because they understood the thought and intention behind the task (Anderson et al., 2013). On the other hand, some students resented being "fed" an assignment's purpose and told why they needed to learn something (Anderson et al., 2013).

To counter these potential challenges, instructors may consider using an inductive or inquiry-based assignment that allows students to discover the purpose for themselves, and encouraging them to think about the logic of the task as it relates to the overall goals of the course (Anderson et al., 2013). Asking students to discover and reflect on the purpose of an assignment and how it connects to the course learning objectives gives students agency in their learning, which may increase engagement (Anderson et al., 2013; Fisher et al., 2016). For example, students might identify the purpose by answering a reflection question about how the assignment relates to the course learning outcomes and how their knowledge or skills will improve through completion of the task.

Steps or Tasks

The TILT framework suggests that the steps of an assignment or activity should be clearly delineated and explained. This requires the instructor to step back and think about any assumptions they may have made about student knowledge and look for opportunities to demystify the assignment by defining terms and explaining processes (see Chapter 8). Providing background about how the steps relate to each other will lead to greater transparency for the students (Winkelmes et al., 2015).

Descriptions of tasks can also include details about any specific methods or techniques students are expected to use. For example, in an online discussion assignment, students might be asked to read articles, watch videos, or review other resources that they can access via links in the course learning management system. If the resources are complex, such as peer-reviewed research articles, it may be useful to provide students with tools that explain how such documents should be read. For example, Harrington (2022) created worksheets that helped students extract the main points from research studies. Next, students might be asked to map out the key ideas of each resource using a synthesis matrix. After developing the necessary foundational knowledge by completing these steps, they might be asked to share their responses to a discussion prompt. Most online discussions require students to interact with their peers in some way, but many students will be uncertain about how to go about this. Therefore, Aloni and Harrington (2018) suggested that instructors should provide clear guidance on all aspects of discussion board participation, including how students should engage with and respond to their peers. For instance, they outlined the benefits of asking and answering Socratic questions and provided a list of examples. Instructors can support students by articulating the component steps of each task, such as accessing resources via a library database and then analyzing them with computer software. It is also useful to mention common mistakes and how to avoid them. Helping students identify what they need to do and providing support and strategies on how to complete the required tasks are important aspects of making assignments more transparent and culturally affirming (see Chapter 2).

Using action verbs based on Bloom's taxonomy (such as "apply," "analyze," "evaluate," and "create") to communicate each step of the assignment will help students understand what is expected of them (TeachThought, 2018). Some of these steps will be formative assessments—mini-assignments such as quizzes, drafts, or sections of a project that are typically required throughout the learning process. These support the student in completing their final, summative assessment (which demonstrates if they have achieved the course learning outcomes) because they comprise a roadmap of the tasks that need to be completed throughout the semester, which enables both the student and the instructor to know if the student is on track with their learning (see Chapter 8). In many cases, instructors will establish a progression of tasks that starts with helping students acquire foundational knowledge before moving on to the development of more complex skills, such as analysis and application (TeachThought, 2018).

The tasks section of an assignment can also provide guidance on the sequence in which tasks should be completed, with an explanation of how the knowledge and skills learned during each task builds on the knowledge and skills learned during the previous tasks. For example, if a student is undertaking a research project, the instructor can provide guidelines that map out the steps that must be completed and in what order. Outlining specific steps in this way, or offering optional "lab" sessions during which students can learn how to complete the required tasks, can help students develop skills and knowledge related to the mechanics of assignments (Mowreader, 2023).

Instructors should also acknowledge that certain tasks will be challenging, and they may encourage students to reflect on their progress as they complete each step or task. Winkelmes et al. (2015) suggested informing students that they are likely to encounter challenges because learning invariably requires effort. Acknowledging these challenges and the frustrations students may experience is an important aspect of transparency. Explaining the purpose of struggle will give students the confidence to persist even in the face of serious challenges (Winkelmes et al., 2015).

Criteria for Success

Instructors should provide detailed explanations of what is expected of students in terms of the end product of an assignment and the grading criteria that will be used to determine the level of success, plus how much weight the assignment grade will carry in the final course grade (Winkelmes, 2013). Harrington and Thomas (2018) suggested illustrating the weighting of all assignments in a pie chart, as this will make it easier for students to understand the relative importance of each task.

The TILT template (TILT Higher Ed, n.d.) encourages instructors to provide students with clear descriptions and definitions of the final product for each assignment, including details of content, extent (e.g., brief summary or longer essay), and format (e.g., MLA or APA). These can be shared via a rubric or demonstrated via examples.

Rubrics

Rubrics are a valuable tool for organizing assignment criteria and providing students with a means to evaluate their assignments. They are also helpful to faculty because they prompt instructors to think carefully about what they want students to demonstrate via the assignment and what components or characteristics are needed. Expressing assignment criteria in a well-organized rubric that defines the task and evaluation method gives instructors a consistent format for assessing student performance. Students are more likely to create desired products when resources such as rubrics are transparently shared (Northern Illinois University Center for Innovative Teaching and Learning, 2012).

Creating a rubric can be time-consuming, but it is a worthwhile investment. Instructors often report that students do not have as many questions when rubrics are provided, and that the final grading process is more straightforward when students submit higher-quality academic products, which is more likely with transparent assignments that include articulated grading criteria (MIT Teaching and Learning Lab, 2023).

There are three main types of rubric: checklist, holistic, and analytical. Each of these has advantages and challenges. The checklist rubric is simply a list of the required components. One key benefit of this rubric is that it is easy to create and easy for students to understand and use. Its principal challenge is that it does not communicate or assess quality; rather, the simple presence or absence of an assignment characteristic or component determines the grade.

A holistic rubric involves an instructor sharing what an A product looks like, as compared to B, C, D, and F grades (DePaul Teaching Commons, 2023). Holistic rubrics are fairly easy to create, though it is sometimes difficult to delineate the differences between the various grade criteria. Therefore, a modified version may involve describing only an A product. Yet, instructors can still find it challenging to use holistic rubrics because students may adequately address certain parts of what is required for an A but miss the mark on others, which can make it difficult to determine the correct grade.

Analytical rubrics are the most comprehensive type of rubric but also the most difficult to create. In an analytical rubric, instructors need to articulate the various components of an assignment and then explain what students need to do for each component to earn different grades (DePaul Teaching Commons, 2023). Differentiating between the various grade levels on numerous components can be challenging, but this type of rubric does provide the greatest transparency. That said, some researchers have suggested that this level of detail may stifle student creativity (To & Carless, 2016). Moreover, students may feel overwhelmed by the wealth of detail and may need help determining the most important elements to include in their final product.

It can be helpful for instructors to choose a rubric type and use it consistently throughout the semester for each assignment, as this can help students understand course expectations (Toy, 2022). Consistency in how the purpose, steps, and grading criteria are shared is another way to increase assignment transparency.

There are many examples of checklist, holistic, and analytical rubrics on teaching and learning center websites. For example, instructors can use the Valid Assessment of Learning in Undergraduate Education (VALUE) rubrics developed by the Association of American Colleges and Universities (2021) as templates for their own rubrics to evaluate student performance. The VALUE rubrics reflect the three principles of transparent assignments: purpose, tasks, and criteria. Instructors may wish to include benchmarks or milestones within their assignments to help students understand the skills and knowledge they will need at the start of their learning journey and as they progress toward graduation (Association of American Colleges and Universities, 2009).

Examples or Models

Examples of assignments can bring the criteria to life and provide a model to help students visualize what the final product should look like (see Chapter 8). For example, Portia Scott shares a model poem before asking students to write their own poem (see Appendix, Example 12). Another approach is to use examples of previous students' work, as these can provide a boost to students' academic confidence, and their belief that they can produce similar outcomes (Dixon et al., 2020). Similarly, if an instructor is teaching a course for the first time, it can be helpful for them to create sample work products to share with students.

It is important to note, however, that presenting a succession of excellent examples can leave students feeling overwhelmed, anxious, and lacking confidence in their ability to achieve similarly outstanding results (Dixon et al., 2020). To avoid this pitfall, instructors should share a range of good work so that every student is able to relate to at least one example, regardless of their level of confidence (Dixon et al., 2020; Lipnevich et al., 2014). In addition, instructors may share examples of lower-quality work and ask students what is missing (Hutchings et al., 2016).

Engaging students in actively evaluating examples and explaining which aspects meet or exceed the criteria and which may be improved can help them develop insights they can apply to their own work (To et al., 2022). Active engagement may include class activities such as peer discussion of the examples, teacher-led interaction, and student presentations of their evaluations (To & Carless, 2016). Students can also compare their own work to the examples. Through these self-reflective processes, students can internalize what successful work looks like so they can apply similar criteria in the future, building their academic self-efficacy (Dixon et al., 2020). Including a self-reflection phase in the assignment also helps students think about how they utilized the examples and managed the assignment tasks. Reflection activities can help students identify their strengths and weaknesses, which in turn enables them to develop improvement plans (To et al., 2022).

When using examples, it is important to explain that they merely illustrate the various ways in which previous students tackled the assignment. Students should be cautioned about modeling their own work too closely on the examples, rather than demonstrating their knowledge in more creative ways. One way to counter this potential challenge is by sharing a range of examples that illustrate the various ways in which the assignment could be approached (Dixon et al., 2020; see also Chapters 5 and 6).

Tools for Creating Transparent Assignments

Transparent assignment design can be applied in any discipline and for many different types of assignment, from those involving written and oral communication to those requiring expressions of quantitative literacy and integrative learning (Peplow et al., 2021). Instructors who wish to make their assignments more transparent should reflect on the assumptions they make about students' prior knowledge and consider the inferences students may have to draw to complete their assignments (Peplow et al., 2021; see also Chapter 2). These exercises will reveal where further detail and clarity may be needed.

The TILT Higher Ed website (https://tilthighered.com) provides instructors, faculty developers, and institutional leaders with numerous templates and examples that can be helpful when creating transparent assignments. Instructors who review the examples on this website should consider which aspects would be most useful to their students and where additional details may be needed. In one of the examples, for instance, there is no statement of purpose and no explanation of how the assignment will support student learning. Moreover, the assignment tasks are buried within extensive background information on the topic, and there are no details about what would comprise a strong submission. Therefore, after viewing this example, many instructors would immediately identify several areas for improvement. By contrast, other examples illustrate some of the most important aspects of transparent assignments, such as purpose statements and clear descriptions of tasks. More transparent assignments enable students to understand what they have to do and why, and check their progress against a list of tasks.

Faculty who are interested in creating transparent assignments may benefit from working in an organized group to evaluate their assignments and determine how to revise them. One example of such a group is the National Institute for Learning Outcomes Assessment (NILOA). On the

NILOA website (www.learningoutcomesassessment.org), there are a series of templates, meeting agendas, and guidelines for transforming the way instructors conceive of and create meaningful, transparent assignments. Instructors who engage in a charrette (a collaborative design workshop) to think about, design, and recreate their assignments can create more equitable pathways for their students (National Institute for Learning Outcomes Assessment, 2023).

Conclusion

Transparent assignments are an effective way for instructors to create equitable learning environments for their students. They do not assume that students have access to some kind of unpublished rule book about higher education. Rather, the transparent approach breaks down the "invisible curriculum" by revealing what may not be obvious to students who lack college knowledge. Research has demonstrated that the TILT framework, which involves sharing the purpose, steps, and grading criteria for assignments, improves motivation, engagement, and retention of underserved college students, including first-generation students, especially in their first year (Peplow et al., 2021). This is because students who know the purpose of an assignment, what is expected of them, and how they will be graded are empowered to take control of their learning.

By elucidating items that have traditionally been relegated to the "hidden curriculum," transparent assignment design minimizes the influence of a student's background on their ability to understand the assignment. This results in improved learning for all and a more equitable learning environment. Therefore, instructors who aim to support the success of all their students are encouraged to make the necessary investment to clarify the purpose of each assignment, the steps or tasks that students will need to complete, and how they will be graded on their submissions.

Reflection Questions

1. How can making my assignments more transparent benefit students? How will I benefit from this process?
2. What do I want students to learn from this assignment and how have I communicated the purpose of the assignment to them?
3. What assumptions might I be making about students' prior knowledge or skills related to understanding this assignment?
4. What characteristics or components of the assignment do I need to define?
5. How will students know what actions they need to take (and in what order) to complete the assignment successfully?

6   How can I more clearly communicate the assignment tasks to students?
7   What type of rubric or grading criteria will work best for this assignment?
8   What examples could I provide to students to help them understand what their final products should look like?

References

Aloni, M., & Harrington, C. (2018). Research-based practices for improving the effectiveness of asynchronous online discussion boards. *Scholarship of Teaching and Learning in Psychology*, 4(4), 271–289.

Anderson, A. D., Hunt, A. N., Powell, R. E., & Brooks Dollar, C. (2013). Student perceptions of teaching transparency. *Journal of Effective Teaching*, 13(2), 38–47.

Angel, R., & Merken, S. (2021). Assessing TILT in a college classroom. *National Teaching and Learning Forum*, 30(4), 1–3.

Association of American Colleges and Universities (2009). Inquiry and analysis VALUE rubric. https://www.aacu.org/initiatives/value-initiative/value-rubrics/value-rubrics-inquiry-and-analysis.

Association of American Colleges and Universities (2021). VALUE ADD: Assignment design and diagnostic tool. https://www.aacu.org/initiatives/value-initiative/assignment-design-and-diagnostic-tool.

Bhavsar, V. M. (2020). A transparent assignment to encourage reading for a flipped course. *College Teaching*, 68(1), 33–44. https://doi.org/10.1080/87567555.2019.1696740.

DePaul Teaching Commons (2023). Types of rubrics. DePaul University Center for Teaching and Learning. https://resources.depaul.edu/teaching-commons/teaching-guides/feedback-grading/rubrics/Pages/types-of-rubrics.aspx.

Dixon H., Hawe, E., & Hamilton, R. (2020). The case for using exemplars to develop academic self-efficacy. *Assessment and Evaluation in Higher Education*, 45(3), 460–471. https://doi.org/10.1080/02602938.2019.1666084.

Fisher, K., Kouyoumdjian, C., Roy, B., Talavera-Bustillo, V., & Willard, M. (2016). Building a culture of transparency. *Peer Review; Washington*, 18(1/2), 8–11. https://www.proquest.com/docview/1805184422.

Harrington, C. (2022). *Student success in college: Doing what works!* (4th ed.). Cengage Learning.

Harrington, C., & Thomas, M. (2018). *Designing a motivational syllabus: Creating a learning path for student engagement*. Stylus Publishing.

Hutchings, P., Jankowski, N. A., & Schultz, K. E. (2016). Designing effective classroom assignments: Intellectual work worth sharing. National Institute for Learning Outcomes Assessment. https://eric.ed.gov/?id=EJ1094146.

Leuzinger, R., & Grallo, J. (2019). Reaching first-generation and underrepresented students through transparent assignment design. *Library Faculty Publications and Presentations*, 11. https://digitalcommons.csumb.edu/lib_fac/11.

Lipnevich, A. A., McCallen, L. N., Miles, K. P., & Smith, J. K. (2014). Mind the gap! Students' use of exemplars and detailed rubrics as formative assessments. *Instructional Science*, 42, 539–559. https://doi.org/10.1007/s11251-013-9299-9.

MIT Teaching and Learning Lab (2023). How to use rubrics. https://tll.mit.edu/teaching-resources/assess-learning/how-to-use-rubrics/.

Mowreader, A. (2023, May 22). Academic success tips: Labs promote better student discussion boards. *Inside Higher Ed.* https://www.insidehighered.com/news/student-success/academic-life/2023/05/22/academic-success-tip-labs-promote-better-student?mc_cid=ac4badb.

National Institute for Learning Outcomes Assessment (2023). Assignment charrette. https://www.learningoutcomesassessment.org/wp-content/uploads/2021/11/Resources_for_Conducting_an_Assignment_Charrette1.pdf.

Northern Illinois University Center for Innovative Teaching and Learning (2012). Rubrics for assessment: An instructional guide for university faculty and teaching assistants. https://www.niu.edu/citl/resources/guides/instructional-guide.

Peplow, A., Carter, J. A., Baumgartner, J., Hennessy, M., Greer, M., Schlembach, S., Mallory, B., & Refaei, B. (2021). Transparent assignment design: A multidisciplinary survey assessing students' perceptions. *Journal for Research and Practice in College Teaching*, 6(1), 61–102. https://journals.uc.edu/index.php/jrpct/article/view/4208.

Sathy, V., & Hogan, K. A. (n.d.). How to make your teaching more inclusive: Advice guide. *Chronicle of Higher Education.* https://www.chronicle.com/article/how-to-make-your-teaching-more-inclusive/?cid=gen_sign_in.

TeachThought (2018). 100+ Bloom's taxonomy verbs for critical thinking. https://www.teachthought.com/critical-thinking/blooms-taxonomy-verbs/.

TILT Higher Ed (n.d.). Checklist for designing transparent assignments. https://tilthighered.com/assets/pdffiles/Checklist%20for%20Designing%20Transparent%20Assignments.pdf.

Toy, C. (2022). Transparent assignments: A proven tool for equity and success. https://clt.champlain.edu/transparent-assignments-a-proven-tool-for-equity-and-success/.

To, J., & Carless, D. (2016). Making productive use of exemplars: Peer discussion and teacher guidance for positive transfer of strategies. *Journal of Further and Higher Education*, 40(6), 746–764. https://doi.org/10.1080/0309877X.2015.1014317.

To, J., Panadero, E., & Carless, D. (2022) A systematic review of the educational uses and effects of exemplars. *Assessment and Evaluation in Higher Education*, 47(8), 1167–1182. https://doi.org/10.1080/02602938.2021.201113.

Winkelmes, M. (2013). Transparency in teaching: Faculty share data and improve student learning. *Liberal Education*, 99(2). https://eric.ed.gov/?id=EJ1094742.

Winkelmes, M., Bernacki, M., Butler, J., Zochowski, M., Golanics, J., & Weavil, K. H. (2016). A teaching intervention that increases underserved college students' success. *Peer Review; Washington*, 8(1/2), 31–36. https://www.proquest.com/docview/1805184428.

Winkelmes, M., Copeland, D. E., Jorgensen, E., Sloat, A., Smedley, A., Pizor, P., Johnson, K., & Jalene, S. (2015). Benefits (some unexpected) of transparently designed assignments. *National Teaching and Learning Forum*, 24(4), 4–6.

Chapter 8

Providing Assignment Support and Feedback

M. Geneva Murray and Robert Scafe

It's a 3000-level online course and Megan cannot wait to have her students start engaging with one another during the first week of class. At the start of the semester, she provided rubrics for each discussion prompt and informed the students that she will be using these rubrics to grade their work. However, as the weeks go by, she realizes that some students are not using the rubrics. She does not understand, as her colleagues told her that the rubrics would be helpful to her students. After reaching out to a few students, she discovers some of them had been instructed on how to use rubrics in a previous class, but most had not and were unsure how to utilize them and apply them to their work. Some students were frustrated, feeling as though they had been asked for too much, too quickly, without the appropriate support, and without timely, constructive feedback that was applicable to future assignments. Others were wondering if they were cut out for higher education at all.

Megan could use a culturally affirming approach (see Chapter 2) to consider what support and feedback should look like in a classroom that is broadly engaged in culturally affirming educational experiences. To provide support, instructors need to be aware of the assets and challenges within their community of learners. They can attend to how students learn by scaffolding assignments and making visible the social-emotional and tacit knowledge aspects of managing a project that are often ignored in assignments and supporting resources. Tacit knowledge refers to knowledge gained from personal or professional experiences. Providing multimodal, specific, and affirming feedback that supports students' growth and sense of academic belonging is equally important.

The Why of Support and Feedback: Helping Students Grow through Assignments

Affirming support and feedback can change the way students experience assignments. Providing high-level support for assignments through skillful teaching practices can help build intrinsic motivation for students and

DOI: 10.4324/9781003443797-9

engage them in deep learning (Ramsden, 1984). Assignment support and feedback processes can also be used to overcome barriers that are detrimental to all—but particularly marginalized—students. Barriers within higher education may contribute to—or instill in—students a feeling that they do not belong and are imposters (Breeze et al., 2022; Murray et al., 2022).

The imposter phenomenon, which is associated with anxiety and a fear of failure, disproportionality affects minoritized students (Parkman, 2016) and is heightened in the first year of study and during high-stakes assignments (Murray et al., 2022). Students may try to manage their fear of failure by avoiding an assignment, withdrawing from in-class activities, or even abandoning the course (Cox, 2009). First-generation students are disproportionately disadvantaged by vague instructions on how to complete assignments successfully—including how to write in disciplinary-specific ways, how to ascertain what information graders are looking for, and how to navigate test formats—because they lack access to information about academic student life (Collier & Morgan, 2007).

Instructors are not always as clear in their instructions as they think because they may view assignments through an expert bias reflective of both explicit and tacit knowledge. We accumulate tacit knowledge through our own lived experiences, which makes it "more difficult to articulate" and explain (Muscanell & Shaffer, 2020, p. 18). Conversely, explicit knowledge is easier to communicate and transfer to others. As experts, we sometimes forget about the tacit knowledge that is required to complete an assignment.

Fortunately, making tacit knowledge visible is an effective way to enhance students' confidence, help them prepare for assessments (Muscanell & Shaffer, 2020), and improve their performance (Rust et al., 2003). Teaching students how to be discussion facilitators (Muscanell & Shaffer, 2020), deliver presentations (Shimo, 2011), hone the social and collaborative skills they need for cooperative learning (Johnson et al., 1994), and evaluate online sources (Breakstone et al., 2021) are all examples of support interventions that improve student performance by highlighting the tacit abilities that content- and skill-focused rubrics might leave unaddressed.

By providing students with a clearer understanding of how to complete an assignment, and not just what an assignment is, instructors can work toward mitigating barriers to student success. In tandem with scaffolding, this may reshape students' experiences of assessment, allow for deeper learning, and mitigate imposter feelings (Cox, 2009). Supporting students with completing assignments and providing feedback improves student self-regulation, academic confidence, retention, and academic achievement (Tuckman & Kennedy, 2011; McGuire & McGuire, 2015).

Approaches to Support

Instructors can take a proactive approach to supporting students with assignments. First, they can explore their students' tacit and background knowledge. Then, they can identify helpful resources and examples. Finally, providing students with opportunities to engage in and learn from formative assessments enables instructors to provide ongoing support and feedback. The next few sections discuss how these support mechanisms contribute to creating a classroom environment that is culturally affirming and meaningful.

Support via Exploring Tacit and Background Knowledge

Instructors can begin by asking themselves: "Will students need to be familiar with any concepts, skills, or knowledge to complete the assignment successfully?" For example, Fritzgerald (2020) described an exam task that assumed students' familiarity with Yellowstone Park. However, the national park was not discussed in class, so the assumption rested on students' ability to travel to Yellowstone or learn about it by some other means. Fritzgerald (2020, p. 92) therefore argued that "there are biases in the way tests are written and assembled" that privilege students who possess "construct-irrelevant" skills and knowledge—defined as those that are unrelated to what is being measured in the summative assessment. It is important for instructors to identify these construct-irrelevant attributes and evaluate their own assumptions about their students' background knowledge.

The process of identifying the tacit knowledge that is needed for an assignment requires removing oneself from the expert role. Muscanell and Shaffer (2020, p. 18) considered this after observing student-led discussions in which, "despite detailed assignment instructions, rubrics, instructor modeling, and planning meetings, students struggled to reach the desired level of performance." An instructional designer helped them identify the tacit knowledge they were using as successful discussion facilitators and create some tools to support the students' acquisition of this skill. As a result, they developed a resource for discussions (see http://bit.ly/greatdiscussions). In other words, it was only by working with someone else that Muscanell and Shaffer were able to recognize the knowledge they possessed and then communicate it to their students.

One excellent way to access tacit knowledge and skills is by conducting a diagnostic survey to ascertain students' familiarity with the knowledge they will need in the course. Instructors can use the findings to develop appropriate supports, including a brief background, a glossary, or other tools that will create the shared understandings that are needed to complete assessments. For example, YouTube videos that provide tips on how to function effectively in a group or how to read and analyze a research study could be shared with students. Instructors could also create their own resources and share these on the syllabus and in the learning management system. For instance, they could create screencasts in which students are shown how to access resources or provide guidelines on how to interact with peers in an online discussion. Such tools can help ensure that student performance is not negatively impacted by unfamiliarity with knowledge that is not directly addressed in the course.

In addition to using diagnostic tools, instructors should encourage students to voice concerns and ask questions. For instance, in the first week, they might urge students to post their responses to the syllabus on an annotation platform such as Hypothes.is or Google Docs, including what they are finding most and least exciting and what might help them feel more connected with the week's content. This type of activity not only helps instructors get to know their students (see Chapter 4) but provides insights into the students' attitudes toward the various assessments and the support they feel they need. This sort of feedback often helps instructors clarify assignment directions and identify additional resources to share.

That said, any strategy that relies on students voicing their concerns obviously privileges those who feel more comfortable coming forward. Students from cultures that value high power distance (or more hierarchical structures) will be less likely to ask for help from their instructor (Wang, 2017), which could deny them the assistance that more vocal students receive. One possible solution is to require *all* students to submit questions or concerns as part of a low-stakes assignment, which should normalize the process of asking for help and clarification. However, although there is value in asking students for feedback, a more equity-based approach would anticipate their questions and needs and proactively provide support to the whole class. This transparent approach to assignments can be especially helpful to students of color and other marginalized populations (see Chapter 7).

Support via Scaffolded Examples

Vygotsky's social learning theory argues that experts can help students progress beyond their capacity by gradually giving them more responsibility for their instructional activities (Vygotsky & Cole, 1978). In this gradual release of responsibility instructional framework (Fisher & Frey, 2021), students will learn more when instructors first demonstrate and then work collaboratively with students before asking them to complete tasks on their own. The following steps could be taken in an assignment:

1   Students are given guided instruction whereby the instructor demonstrates what needs to be achieved and precisely how the instructor would achieve it.

2   Moving slowly and intentionally toward more independence, the whole class, with the aid of the instructor, completes the task, providing one another with feedback.
3   The instructor becomes progressively less involved as the students work collaboratively to achieve the objective with peer support and feedback.
4   The students work independently to complete their assessments, and the instructor is in a much more supportive role through feedback and assessment.

Another type of scaffold is when instructors provide exemplars of completed assignments. Providing multiple exemplars that show different tiers of student work, when combined with guidance about how to use them (Hawe et al., 2019), is an effective means of supporting students. Instructors may even create their own examples or models, as Kelsie Potter encourages them to do in an assignment that asks students to design their own pride flag (see Appendix, Example 4). To and Carless (2016) detailed several ways in which instructors can engage students with exemplars to ensure proper scaffolding of the exercise, such as requiring students to peer review and discuss the exemplars, leading a class discussion about them, and assigning brief group presentations on how students would improve them. Instructors may also provide the exemplars with annotations, which could then be discussed with students. These annotations would provide a window into the instructor's expectations so the students see feedback before submitting their work, as opposed to only afterward. These strategies help in distinguishing exemplars from "model" assignments, which Handley and Williams (2011) warn may result in students imitating the example rather than creatively engaging with the assignment. Additionally, students will learn to use the rubric for assignments to greater effect, creating an opportunity for self-assessment of their work using the rubric.

Support via Formative Assessments

Instructors can also provide support through course design that relies heavily on formative assessments (see Chapter 1). These small, low-stakes assignments can culminate over time into a larger assignment. Over the course of a semester, students may be tasked with assignments that build slowly on their knowledge and skills, and therefore increase in difficulty at a rate appropriate to the students' progress. The students receive feedback on each formative assessment submission from their instructor and/or their peers, which they can then integrate into the final summative assessment. This "feedforward" approach keeps feedback relevant so students are motivated to act upon it (Glover & Brown, 2006). Students have shared that feedback on formative assessments helps them develop confidence as well as skills (Harrington, 2021).

It can also be helpful to have students write a reflection on the key pieces of formative feedback they received throughout the semester and how this helped them shape their final project. This reflection component focuses student attention on their learning process and the growth they have achieved (see Chapter 3).

Support via Connections to Campus Resources

Instructors need to be mindful that students may need non-academic support during assignments. Anxiety, confusion, and lack of confidence related to assignments can negatively impact a student's performance. Stress and mental health challenges can also impact academic outcomes. Indeed, in a national student survey, 30.7 percent of all respondents—and 52.6 percent of trans or gender non-conforming respondents—reported ongoing anxiety in the last year that negatively impacted their academic performance (American College Health Association, 2022). Self-doubt may be amplified by stereotype threat or the imposter phenomenon.

Instructors should assume that many students have had direct, personal experience with discrimination, oppression, and/or trauma, or that they are close to someone who has had such experiences. Carello and Butler (2014, p. 157) cited studies showing that, "by the time youth reach college, 66% to 85% report lifetime traumatic event exposure." Therefore, assignments that intersect with difficult experiences in the lives of students may require types of assessment support that differ from those that instructors typically view as supportive. For example, instructors might consider distributing an anonymous survey to students before the first day of class that details the sensitive topics that will be discussed, with guidance on how support will be provided to students as they engage with these topics (see Appendix, Example 1).

Instructors have typically not been trained to help students manage stress that might impact their ability to complete assignments. Moreover, even if an instructor has received training, it is important for them not to take on the role of counselor. That said, it is helpful for instructors to familiarize themselves with online and on-campus resources, including counseling, so that they can normalize the process of accessing these resources for students. Instructors may also want to add supportive language to their syllabi, such as: "You deserve support. If you are experiencing issues such as bias, gender-based violence, or financial stress that are impacting your ability to focus on your learning, I encourage you to connect with the following resources ..." In short, students need to know that they are not alone, and help is available.

Providing Assignment Feedback

Assignment support requires instructors to provide students with feedback. But not all feedback is created equal. Effective feedback requires building a trusting relationship with students (see Chapter 4) so they will be more inclined to listen to the instructor's suggestions and understand that feedback represents a belief in their ability to improve. This involves more than simply providing encouraging feedback, however. In fact, there is evidence that students routinely ignore vague praise (Ackerman & Gross, 2010; Cionea et al., 2022), or even that it may trigger stereotype threat among marginalized students who interpret patronizing commentary as confirmation of the instructor's bias (Cohen & Steele, 2002). Striking the right balance between praise and correction can be challenging, but the wise feedback approach articulated by Cohen and Steele (2002, p. 311) shows the way: instructors should tell students about their high expectations, that their feedback is designed to support them in meeting those high expectations, and that the whole class has the "capacity to reach those standards."

Unfortunately, though, students often lack opportunities to learn from feedback. For example, Taras (2006) reported that undergraduate students are not typically granted opportunities to "revise and resubmit" on the basis of feedback, whereas graduate students and professionals are afforded these opportunities more often. As Taras provocatively pointed out, it is only fair and reasonable that academics should afford their students the same iterative feedback cycle that they themselves enjoy during the publishing process.

Characteristics of Useful Feedback

The quality of feedback matters. It is most helpful when it is prompt, asset-based, positively phrased, instructive, specific, and focused on the purpose of the assignment. Instructors are not the only ones who are capable of providing useful feedback; peers can do it too with the right support.

Prompt

For feedback to be part of any learning cycle, it must arrive in good time to benefit students as they work on their next assignment. In Beaumont and colleagues' study, one student commented: "We had no feedback from the other essay that we handed in ... so how are we meant to write [the] big essay without the feedback from the small one?" (Beaumont et al., 2011, p. 679). Unfortunately, many students have stressed that they had no idea how well they were doing in a course because feedback was infrequent, often based only on summative rather than formative assessments, and rarely timely. Even if instructors create assignments that build on previous tasks, the benefits are lost when students receive no feedback and are therefore denied the opportunity for improvement.

Providing affirming, instructive, and specific feedback at the *end* of a course obviously does not support students in their development *during* the course. Instructors are therefore encouraged to set aside time for grading and providing high-quality feedback promptly. One effective approach is calendar blocking shortly after assignment due dates to free up sufficient time for this important part of the learning process.

Asset Based

An asset-based approach to feedback is foundational in creating an environment in which feedback can be received productively. Indeed, it is about encouraging student growth in areas where they can improve while honoring their progress in the learning process. Instructors are encouraged to name the unique assets that students are bringing to any given assignment, amplifying those that they shared with them (see Chapter 4). To be clear, this does not mean issuing praise regardless of performance. To build trust, affirmative feedback must be both specific and merited; otherwise, it may be dismissed as patronizing fluff or confirmation of the instructor's prejudices (Cohen & Steele, 2002).

Hammond's (2015) "asset-based feedback protocol" is a good example of the wise feedback approach to blending high standards with growth-oriented feedback. In this approach, instructors develop relationships through the feedback process by meeting with students to learn more about them, discover which aspects of the assignment they found easy and more challenging, and observe their responses to feedback. At various stages throughout each meeting, the instructor will affirm the student's capacity to achieve success by emphasizing what they have accomplished so far and encouraging them to make further progress. Engaging with students about what they are doing well not only validates them but also helps them build on their achievements. If instructors struggle to find the time to meet with all their students individually, they can use an asset-based approach when delivering feedback via periodic emails or the learning management system. One such example of asset-based feedback is as follows:

> Your perspective here really added a lot of value to the course material. I appreciate you sharing about the resources in our community and how we can understand this topic through a more local lens. I appreciate how you've used the course materials in conjunction with your personal experiences. Keep doing this!

Positively Phrased and Growth Focused

Comments that are phrased positively render students more receptive to the feedback, regardless of whether its content is affirmative or corrective. For example, Cionea and colleagues demonstrated that students perceived their teaching assistants as more competent, trustworthy, and benevolent when they made comments such as "the paper needed better organization" as opposed to "the paper did not have good organization" (Cionea et al., 2023, pp. 593–594). The first of these comments opens a portal to future improvement, whereas the second comment's final judgment slams it shut.

Feedback that helps students develop a growth mindset can be especially valuable (see Chapter 3). If students have faced bias or been denied growth-oriented feedback in previous institutions, they may have internalized a fixed mindset where they believe that they, and their capacity to learn, are the issue (Hammond, 2015). In tandem with encouraging a growth mindset, instructors can affirm students' abilities as linked to the assignment's tasks. Luke Wood emphasized the importance of validating capacity when working with Black men who may have been denied this recognition previously (cited in Hilton, 2017). Newman and colleagues also encouraged instructors to validate Black male students' ability with statements such as "you can succeed" as this can foster a sense of belonging (Newman et al., 2015, p. 571). Therefore, instructors are encouraged to validate student ability and effort to encourage a growth mindset. In their study of undergraduate exam performance in a large introductory psychology course, Bostwick and Becker-Blease (2018) found a significant improvement for students who received a growth mindset message that communicated that new skills can be learned and encouraged persistence and hard work after their first exam. Seemingly minor changes in phrasing can convey a growth mentality that improves student receptivity to comments.

In many cases, a positive approach can be used even if the goal is corrective in nature. In other words, positive feedback can be used to encourage improvements as well as validate excellent work. In Figure 8.1 the instructor provided only negative feedback after the writer failed to provide an attribution for quotations, whereas in Figure 8.2 positive feedback on one part of the assignment was used to encourage the student to improve another part.

In the first iteration (Figure 8.1), it is easy to envision the instructor sighing in exasperation. As a result, the student who reads the comments may feel that the instructor has lost hope in them, which could leave them feeling deflated and reluctant to ask for support in the future. Conversely, in the second iteration (Figure 8.2), the feedback is much more motivational and constructive. After identifying the places where the student has achieved the learning outcome, the instructor uses this success to guide the student to where they might improve. This type of feedback

> The media often blunts the critical power of youth music subcultures by making their rebellion seem cute and harmless. This belittling of musical protest is particularly bad when it comes to female artists. For example, a *Newsweek* story about the Riot Grrrl movement in the 1990's described the feminist musicians as "boldly ideological, but with a mushy warm spot for cute skater boys." This reference to heterosexual teen romance assures the readers of *Newsweek* that Riot Grrrl isn't a serious movement because its feminist rebels just want a "cute skater boy" like typical American teenage girls. In this way, "the Other can be trivialized, naturalized, domesticated" (Hebdige 97). Still, female rockers have proven that they can compete and brush off the sexism in the music industry. "It's based on talent. And so there's not greater and more delicious luxury than being a lady rock star" (Love 164). You can't let the biases of (usually male) music critics determine your value as an artist.

Orphan quote

Another orphan quote. We went over this in class.

Figure 8.1 Only Negative Feedback

> The media often blunts the critical power of youth music subcultures by making their rebellion seem cute and harmless. This belittling of musical protest is particularly bad when it comes to female artists. For example, a *Newsweek* story about the Riot Grrrl movement in the 1990's described the feminist musicians as "boldly ideological, but with a mushy warm spot for cute skater boys." This reference to heterosexual teen romance assures the readers of *Newsweek* that Riot Grrrl isn't a serious movement because its feminist rebels just want a "cute skater boy" like typical American teenage girls. In this way, "the Other can be trivialized, naturalized, domesticated" (Hebdige 97). Still, female rockers have proven that they can compete and brush off the sexism in the music industry. "It's based on talent. And so there's not greater and more delicious luxury than being a lady rock star" (Love 164). You can't let the biases of (usually male) music critics determine your value as an artist.

Great job writing a lead-in that gives key info. about this quote. Now, do that for the two "orphan quotes" marked below: who is speaking? What's the relevant context?

Figure 8.2 Positive Feedback to Improve Another Section of the Assignment

is more open-ended, too. By using guiding questions, the instructor encourages the student not only to edit their work but also to engage in dialogue to discover the answer for themselves.

Specific and Constructive

Providing culturally affirming feedback on assignments means that students are also provided with direction on how to improve. Feedback is most effective when there is sufficient detail (Cionea et al., 2022) and when it connects explicitly to the assignment and course goals (Ackerman & Gross, 2010). Cionea et al. (2022) have shown that affirmatively phrased comments with detailed suggestions for improvement are received better than those that simply suggest the possibility of growth.

Students' enhanced receptivity to specific, actionable feedback underscores the importance of limiting instructor comments to learning goals that are explicitly on the table for the assignment (or course) in question. As Ackerman and Gross (2010, p. 179) have suggested, the quantity of commentary (whether positive or negative) can cause students to disengage, so it is advisable to "decide in advance which one or two lessons are most important" for the assignment, or for the individual student at the time. Simply sharing feedback via a rubric is insufficient. Unless instructors create an ongoing feedback dialogue, students' ability to carry forward the rubric-based feedback to future assignments will be quite limited (Crisp, 2007).

Fosters Self-Correction through Multimodal, Conversational Commenting

Instructors often make corrections when providing feedback. Although modeling when giving feedback can be helpful in some cases, corrections are usually technical in nature. In a study that evaluated 30 undergraduate students' portfolios that contained all their assignments and related feedback from throughout their college careers, Stern and Solomon (2006) found that most of the feedback was related to grammar, punctuation, paragraph or sentence structure, and word choice, with scholarly advice given on only 6 percent of the assignments. This seems to confirm Williams's (1981) suggestion that many instructors approach feedback with an error-hunting mentality. Yet, corrections of grammatical and syntactical errors are not only less helpful than focused feedback on content but time-consuming. Therefore, instructors should save their valuable time and refer students to writing centers on campus for development of these technical skills (Willingham, 1990; Glover & Brown, 2006).

A more productive approach is conversational commenting, which encourages self-correction. Bean (2011) suggested several practices that facilitate this kind of generous, interactive feedback between instructor and student. For example, the instructor might play the naive reader for the student writer, offering "readerly" reactions such as "Whoa, you lost me here" or "Your reader needs a transition here" (Bean, 2011, p. 325). Such real-time marginal reactions create a sense of audience for students and put revision in their hands rather than simply providing a correction. Bean also encouraged instructors to write a summative comment focused on their overall interest in the student's ideas. Through positive and conversational feedback, instructors can overcome the habit of editing and instead help students develop important skills. They should also be mindful not to let comments on minor issues visually overwhelm substantive feedback on higher-order disciplinary skills and concepts that are central to the assignment's purpose. Conversational commenting can be especially beneficial for students of color who have been most marginalized by grammar policing (Inoue, 2015).

Another important tactic related to conversational feedback draws on the audio and audiovisual modes of commentary that are increasingly available to instructors through learning management systems. In her review of research on student reception of multimodal feedback, Wilkinson (2013) argued that audiovisual comments—which have demonstrated utility for students with conditions such as dyslexia—should be part of every inclusive teaching toolkit. Studies have suggested that, in comparison with written feedback, audio and audiovisual comments engage students at a more personal level by nuancing and contextualizing the instructor's suggestions for improvement and eliminating potential difficulties with the instructor's handwriting (Wilkinson, 2013, p. 4). The personal connections established by multimodal feedback can result in students feeling appreciated, which in turn can increase the likelihood of them welcoming and using the feedback. As Grigoryan (2017, p. 462) has shown, audio-visual feedback "may have helped students construct knowledge through the social and cultural interaction with the instructor," confirming the usefulness of Vygotsky's socio-cultural theory as a culturally affirming pedagogy. Happily, these studies have also found that audio feedback may be more efficient, requiring, for example, 12–15 minutes per student, as opposed to the 30 minutes required for written feedback (Knauf, 2016).

Peer Feedback

Feedback need not come from instructors alone; peers can also provide useful suggestions. Well-structured peer review benefits not only the recipient but also the reviewer(s), who learn by actively articulating how rubric criteria apply to concrete situations in their fellow student's work. That said, social feedback can perpetuate inequity. For example, studies have found that peer evaluation can reproduce systemic biases stemming from assumptions about the leadership qualities of women (Meadows & Sekaquaptewa, 2013), high-status groups (Chiu, 2000), and racialized students (Thondhlana & Belluigi, 2017). In other words, students' stereotypes may create inequities in the peer-review process.

Instructors can avoid these pitfalls by designing their approach strategically to help students see the value in one another's contributions. Because learning is social, peer feedback can be an excellent way to emphasize the attributes that each student brings into the classroom and how they can benefit from one another's knowledge and skills. A robust feedback cycle, including peer review, allows students to "develop concepts of standards and criteria" (Taras, 2006, p. 366). Peer feedback also creates a more genuine sense of audience feedback than students would acquire from instructor comments alone. As Taylor (2018) suggested, simulating audiences and realistic scenarios give students a sense that their work has power and makes it more socially relevant, potentially to a student's own identity and circumstances.

Providing feedback can be challenging even for instructors, so it is not surprising that students often feel overwhelmed when asked to critique a peer's work, which usually leads to poor-quality feedback. One solution to this problem is Facey's (2011) "conveyer-belt" peer-review system, an in-class exercise in which each student's paper is passed through a series of small groups, each of which is responsible for a specific feedback task. For example, the first group might focus on the use of quotes, the second on how well the writer has presented their main idea, and the third on whether citations were used appropriately. By the end of the cycle, each group has provided feedback on a single aspect of the paper and the writer receives a comprehensive and credible review from their peers.

David Carless (2002) designed a "mini-viva" (after *viva-voce*—oral exams in the UK educational system) in which fellow students interview the writer of a paper using a series of predetermined conversational questions, such as "Can you back this up?" and "What do you mean by …?" These help the interviewers focus their inquiries on meaningful, higher-order issues in the text. As Facey (2011) pointed out, establishing an iterative "cycle of feedback" through the use of such techniques creates a dialogue around the revision criteria, such that instructor feedback on later drafts functions more as a reminder of what has been discussed in peer review rather than first-time instruction.

As mentioned earlier, although high-quality peer review can harness a conversational ethos to make formative assessment more accessible, countervailing forces in group work can perpetuate inequities for women, racialized groups, and students of lower socio-economic status. In a study of engineering undergraduates, for example, Meadows and Sekaquaptewa (2013) noted that women were often relegated to supporting roles within groups that were not organized in a manner that valued their contributions. Moreover, the students' evaluation of their "self-efficacy" in group work impacted their confidence and ability to carry out tasks. In peer-review groups, this could mean that students who are perceived as leaders will receive the greatest benefit from the feedback process, while those who have the most to gain from a leadership role will benefit the least. One potential solution to this problem may be to adopt a more structured peer-review process featuring designated expert roles. In the context of a STEM classroom, one study found that a "Jigsaw" approach to collaboration significantly reduced students' perception of inequality during group work, which should have a positive impact on both self-evaluation and performance (Theobald et al., 2017).

To back up a bit, though, it seems that building a classroom culture of reciprocity and mutual respect is the most sustainable solution to the problem of feedback-induced inequity. Even before the feedback cycle begins, instructors can invite students to connect their own "conversational moves" in class discussions to substantive and respectful academic citations (Graff et al., 2021). As Anne Curzan (2014) has suggested, linking students' vernacular expressions such as "Piggybacking on what X said" or "Going off what Y said" to academic references can humanize scholarly discourse and help students appreciate the intellectual value of listening and rephrasing, affirming (where possible), and replying.

Once the values of respectful listening and affirmative critique are established, instructors can structure a feedback cycle that capitalizes on the power of authentic reader response. Instructors can model this approach by practicing affirmative and specific phrasing, using the positive to frame the critical, and modeling "readerly" and multimodal feedback. Then, when they ask students to form groups for peer review, they can structure these activities so they offer all students a variety of leadership and expert roles and experiences. In this way, instructors can foster self-evaluation as students internalize the habits of specific and generous feedback they have practiced with their peers.

Reflecting on Feedback Activities

Adding a reflection component to an assignment requirement can ensure that all students read and use the feedback provided. Requiring students to revise work on the basis of feedback is one effective approach. Students have reported that their interest in feedback increases when they are required to use it immediately to revise their work (Harrington, 2021). In addition to having students complete assignments that build upon one another, thus necessitating that they use the feedback received during the next assignment, other approaches, such as exam or assignment wrappers, require reflection on their metacognition so that they can improve their assignment and exam approaches in the future. After an assignment is returned, instructors can ask students to consider how they approached the assignment, what they believe was successful, and what they believe they could do better or differently next time. Providing question prompts about the feedback process can also be helpful. For example, students who worked in small groups as part of a project could be asked to reflect using the following questions as a guide:

- What are one or two highlights that you learned from your peers in the small group discussions?
- What did you learn about yourself from your participation in the small group discussions?
- What skills do you want to develop by practicing more in the next small group?
- What skills are you proud of demonstrating in this small group?
- What feedback did your group receive that will be most helpful for you in your next small group?
- What feedback is still unclear to you? What steps will you take to clarify this feedback?

There are numerous exam and assignment wrapper templates online; instructors can explore what will work best for their students. Exam wrappers are most effective in improving student metacognition when used in multiple classes in one semester (Soicher & Gurung, 2017), so it may be beneficial to require reflection assignments after all or most assessments.

Conclusion

Students benefit from instructor support related to their assignments. This support can be provided in a variety of ways, including acknowledging the tacit knowledge that is needed and helping students gain this knowledge before they start the assignment, sharing examples or models with students, building numerous formative assessments into the course design so students can receive feedback as they complete different parts of a final assignment, and helping students connect to resources as needed. One of the most powerful ways to support learning is through high-quality feedback on assignments. Instructors who want to support their students through feedback are encouraged to block out time on their calendars so they can provide prompt feedback, focus on student assets and strengths, and use positively phrased language. In addition, instructors will want to ensure that feedback is specific and focused on what students can do to improve, and that it fosters self-correction, so students learn how to revise and improve their own work. Instructors are also encouraged to add a reflection component to assignments, requiring students to consider the feedback they have received and how they may use it to improve their knowledge and skills.

Reflection Questions

1. What assumptions have you made about students' prior knowledge?
2. What type of scaffolds can you provide to create equitable learning environments?

3. How can you use models to support student achievement on assignments?
4. How can you help students who need support connect to campus resources?
5. What type of formative assessments can you incorporate into your course?
6. What strategies can you use to provide prompt feedback to students on assignments?
7. What are some examples of feedback that is asset-based?
8. How can you use positively phrased feedback even when students need to make improvements?
9. In what ways can you make your feedback more specific and constructive?
10. What would conversational feedback look like on your assignments, and how can you provide this type of feedback in a multimodal way?
11. In what ways can you build peer feedback on assignments into your course, and how can you support students with providing valuable feedback?
12. What type of reflective components to an assignment could you require to ensure that students are reading, understanding, and benefiting from feedback?

References

Ackerman, D. S., & Gross, B. L. (2010). Instructor feedback: How much do students really want? *Journal of Marketing Education*, 32(2), 172–181. https://doi.org/10.1177/0273475309360159.

American College Health Association (2022). National college health assessment III: Fall 2021: Reference group executive summary. https://www.acha.org/documents/ncha/NCHA-III_FALL_2021_REFERENCE_GROUP_EXECUTIVE_SUMMARY.pdf.

Bean, J., (2011). *Engaging ideas: The professor's guide to integrating writing, critical thinking, and active learning in the classroom* (2nd ed.). Jossey-Bass.

Beaumont, C., O'Doherty, M., & Shannon, L. (2011). Reconceptualizing assessment feedback: A key to improving student learning? *Studies in Higher Education*, 36(6), 671–687. https://doi.org/10.1080/03075071003731135.

Bostwick, K., & Becker-Blease, K. (2018). Quick, easy mindset intervention can boost academic achievement in large introductory psychology classes. *Psychology Learning and Teaching*, 17(2), 177–193. https://doi.org/10.1177/1475725718766426.

Breakstone, J., Smith, M., Connors, P., Ortega, T., Kerr, D., & Wineburg, S. (2021, February 23). Lateral reading: College students learn to critically evaluate internet sources in an online course. *Harvard Kennedy School Misinformation Review*. https://doi.org/10.37016/mr-2020-56.

Breeze, M., Addison, M., & Taylor, Y. (2022). Situating imposter syndrome in higher education. In M. Addison, M. Breeze, & Y. Taylor (Eds.), *The Palgrave handbook of imposter syndrome in higher education* (pp. 1–16). Palgrave.

Carello, J., & Butler, L. D. (2014). Potentially perilous pedagogies: Teaching trauma is not the same as trauma-informed teaching. *Journal of Trauma and Dissociation*, 15(2), 153–168. https://doi.org/10.1080/15299732.2014.867571.

Carless, D. (2002). The "mini-viva" as a tool to enhance assessment for learning. *Assessment and Evaluation in Higher Education*, 27(4), 353–363. https://doi.org/10.1080/0260293022000001364.

Chiu, M. M. (2000). Effects of status on solutions, leadership, and evaluations during group problem solving. *Sociology of Education*, 73(3), 175–195. https://psycnet.apa.org/doi/10.2307/2673215.

Cionea, I. A., Gilmore, B., Machette, A. T., & Kavya, P. (2023). How students respond to critical feedback from teaching assistants: The effect of instructor and feedback characteristics on perceptions of credibility, efficacy, affect, and self-esteem. *Western Journal of Communication*, 87(4), 578–600. https://doi.org/10.1080/10570314.2022.2135386.

Cohen, G. L., & Steele, C. M. (2002). A barrier of mistrust: How negative stereotypes affect cross-race mentoring. In J. Aronson (Ed.), *Improving academic achievement: Impact of psychological factors on education* (pp. 303–327). Academic Press.

Collier, P. J., & Morgan, D. L. (2007). "Is that paper really due today?" Differences in first-generation and traditional college students' understandings of faculty expectations. *Higher Education*, 55, 425–446. https://doi.org/10.1007/s10734-007-9065-5.

Cox, R. D. (2009). "It was just that I was afraid": Promoting success by addressing students' fear of failure. *Community College Review*, 37(1), 52–80. https://doi.org/10.1177/0091552109338390.

Crisp, B. (2007). Is it worth the effort? How feedback influences students' subsequent submission of assessable work. *Assessment and Evaluation in Higher Education*, 32(5), 571–581. https://doi.org/10.1080/02602930601116912.

Curzan, A. (2014, August 7) Humanizing academic citation. *Chronicle of Higher Education*. https://www.chronicle.com/blogs/linguafranca/humanizing-academic-citation.

Facey, J. (2011). "A is for assessment" … strategies for A-level marking to motivate and enable students of all abilities to progress. *Teaching History*, 144, 36–43.

Fisher, D., & Frey, N. (2021). *Better learning through structured teaching*. Association for Supervision & Curriculum Development.

Frieden, J. E. (n.d.) Asset-building assessment: From degrading rubrics to actionable feedback guides. Make Them Master It. https://makethemmasterit.com/2019/08/06/asset-building-assessment/.

Fritzgerald, A. (2020). *Antiracism and universal design for learning*. CAST Professional Publishing.

Glover, C., & Brown, E. (2006). Written feedback for students: Too much, too detailed or too incomprehensible to be effective? *Bioscience Education*, 7(1), 1–16. https://doi.org/10.3108/beej.2006.07000004.

Graff, G., Birkenstein, C., & Durst, R. K. (2021). *"They say/I say": The moves that matter in academic writing with readings* (5th ed.). W. W. Norton & Company.

Grigoryan, A. (2017). Feedback 2.0 in online writing instruction: Combining audio-visual and text-based commentary to enhance student revision and writing competency. *Journal of Computing in Higher Education*, 29(3), 451–476. https://doi.org/10.1007/s12528-017-9152-2.

Hammond, Z. (2015). *Culturally responsive teaching and the brain: Promoting authentic engagement and rigor among culturally and linguistically diverse students*. Corwin Press.

Handley, K., & Williams, L. (2011). From copying to learning: Using exemplars to engage students with assessment criteria and feedback. *Assessment and Evaluation in Higher Education*, 36(1), 95–108. https://doi.org/10.1080/02602930903201669.

Harrington, C. (2021). *Keeping us engaged: Student perspectives (and research-based evidence) on what works and why*. Routledge.

Hawe, E., Lightfoot, U., & Dixon, H. (2019). First-year students working with exemplars: Promoting self-efficacy, self-monitoring and self-regulation. *Journal of Further and Higher Education*, 43(1), 30–44. https://doi.org/10.1080/0309877X.2017.1349894.

Hilton, A. A. (2017, November 16). Prominent scholar calls growth mindset a "cancerous" idea, in isolation. *Huffington Post*. https://www.huffpost.com/entry/prominent-scholar-calls-growth-mindset-a-cancerous_b_5a07f046e4b0f1dc729a6bc3.

Inoue, A. B. (2015). *Antiracist writing assessment ecologies: Teaching and assessing writing for a socially just future*. The WAC Clearinghouse.

Johnson, D. W., Johnson, R. T., & Holubec, E. J. (1994). *The new circles of learning: Cooperation in the classroom and school*. Association for Supervision and Curriculum Development.

Knauf, H. (2016). Reading, listening, and feeling: Audio feedback as a component of an inclusive learning culture at universities. *Assessment and Evaluation in Higher Education*, 41(3), 442–449. http://dx.doi.org/10.1080/02602938.2015.1021664.

McGuire, S. Y., & McGuire, S. (2015). *Teach students how to learn: Strategies you can incorporate into any course to improve student metacognition, study skills, and motivation*. Routledge.

Meadows, L. A., & Sekaquaptewa, D. (2013). *The influence of gender stereotypes on role adoption in student teams*. 120th ASSE Annual Conference and Exposition, June. https://peer.asee.org/22602.

Murray, Ó. M., Chiu, Y. L. T., Wong, B., & Horsburgh, J. (2022). Deindividualizing imposter syndrome: Imposter work among marginalized STEM undergraduates in the UK. *Sociology*, 57(4). https://doi.org/10.1177/00380385221117380.

Muscanell, N., & Shaffer, S. (2020). Breaking it down and building them up: Helping students develop discussion skills in an upper-level seminar course. *Transformative Dialogues: Teaching and Learning Journal*, 13(1), 17–33.

Newman, C. B., Wood, J. L., & Harris, F., III (2015). Black men's perceptions of sense of belonging with faculty members in community colleges. *Journal of Negro Education*, 84(4), 564–577. https://doi.org/10.7709/jnegroeducation.84.4.0564.

Parkman, A. (2016). The imposter phenomenon in higher education: Incidence and impact. *Journal of Higher Education Theory and Practice*, 16(1), 51–60.

Price, M., Handley, K., Millar, J., & O'Donovan, B. (2010). Feedback: All that effort, but what is the effect? *Assessment and Evaluation in Higher Education*, 35(3), 277–289. https://doi.org/10.1080/02602930903541007.

Ramsden, P. (1984). The context of learning in academic departments. In F. Marton, D. Hounsell, & N. Entwistle (Eds.), *The experience of learning* (pp. 144–164). Scottish Academic Press.

Rust, C., Price, M., & O'Donovan, B. (2003). Improving students' learning by developing their understanding of assessment criteria and processes. *Assessment and Evaluation in Higher Education*, 28(2), 147. https://doi.org/10.1080/02602930301671.

Shimo, E. (2011). Implications for effective ways of conducting and assessing presentations in EFL classes. *Language Education in Asia*, 2(2), 227–236. http://dx.doi.org/10.5746/LEiA/11/V2/I2/A05/Shimo.

Soicher, R. N., & Gurung, R. A. (2017). Do exam wrappers increase metacognition and performance? A single course intervention. *Psychology Learning and Teaching*, 16(1), 64–73. https://doi-org.ezproxy.lib.ou.edu/10.1177/1475725716661872.

Stern, L. A., & Solomon, A. (2006). Effective faculty feedback: The road less traveled. *Assessing Writing*, 11(1), 22–41. https://doi.org/10.1016/j.asw.2005.12.001.

Taras, M. (2006). Do unto others or not: Equity in feedback for undergraduates. *Assessment and Evaluation in Higher Education*, 31(3), 365–377. https://doi.org/10.1080/02602930500353038.

Taylor, K. (2018). Culturally relevant writing pedagogy: An investigation of assessments, feedback, and equity. Doctoral dissertation, University of Illinois at Chicago.

Theobald, E. J., Eddy, S. L., Grunspan, D. Z., Wiggins, B. L., & Crowe, A. J. (2017). Student perception of group dynamics predicts individual performance: Comfort and equity matter. *PLoS ONE*, 12(7). https://doi.org/10.1371/journal.pone.0181336.

Thondhlana, G., & Belluigi, D. (2017). Students' reception of peer assessment of group-work contributions: Problematics in terms of race and gender emerging from a South African case study. *Assessment and Evaluation in Higher Education*, 42(7), 1118–1131. https://doi.org/10.1080/02602938.2016.1235133.

To, J., & Carless, D. (2016). Making productive use of exemplars: Peer discussion and teacher guidance for positive transfer of strategies. *Journal of Further and Higher Education*, 40(6), 746–764. https://doi.org/10.1080/0309877X.2015.1014317.

Tuckman, B. W., & Kennedy, G. J. (2011). Teaching learning strategies to increase success of first-term college students. *Journal of Experimental Education*, 79(4), 478–504. https://doi.org/10.1080/00220973.2010.512318.

Vygotsky, L. S., & Cole, M. (1978). *Mind in society: Development of higher psychological processes*. Harvard University Press.

Wang, M. (2017). Designing online courses that effectively engage learners from diverse cultural backgrounds. *British Journal of Educational Technology*, 38(2), 294–311. https://psycnet.apa.org/doi/10.1111/j.1467-8535.2006.00626.x.

Wilkinson, S. (2013). Incorporating audio feedback to enhance inclusivity of courses. *Journal of Learning Development in Higher Education*, 6, 1–7. https://doi.org/10.47408/jldhe.v0i6.218.

Williams, J. M. (1981). The phenomenology of error. *College Composition and Communication*, 32(2), 152–168. https://doi.org/10.2307/356689.

Willingham, D. B. (1990). Effective feedback on written assignments. *Teaching of Psychology*, 17(1), 10–13.

Appendix
Assignment Examples from the Field

There are many ways instructors can apply the principles that make assignments culturally affirming and meaningful, as described by Martin (Chapter 2) and Arend and Carlson (Chapter 3). Instructors representing different types of institutions and teaching across a variety of disciplines have provided examples of assignments that they believe are culturally affirming and meaningful. To model transparency, as described by Wasserman and Ayeni (Chapter 7), these assignment examples include purpose and task sections. Due to space limitations, criteria for grading—the third component of transparent assignments—were not provided in the examples, but these would typically be shared with students. Each instructor also explained why they believe the assignment is culturally affirming and meaningful.

It is hoped that these examples will provide instructors striving to create more inclusive classroom learning environments with ideas about how to modify current assignments or develop new ones. The first five assignment examples will help instructors get to know their students, and students get to know one another. These can be easily modified for use in a variety of disciplines. The rest of the Appendix consists of assignment examples for each of three broad disciplines: Science and Allied Health, Arts and Humanities, and Education. These are not meant to be considered as perfect templates; rather, they simply represent instructors' efforts to create more culturally affirming and meaningful assignments for their students.

Getting to Know Your Students Assignments

Example 1: Exploring Support Needs via a Survey by M. Geneva Murray

Name of Course: Creating Social Change

PURPOSE

- To provide students with information about the topics that will be discussed in class, and how the instructor hopes to support students as they engage in the learning tasks.

- To determine what types of supports students may feel they need throughout the semester.
- To help the instructor determine if current support plans need to be expanded or modified to help students achieve success.

TASK

It should be noted that this survey was adapted from a resource developed by the University of Oklahoma's Center for Faculty Excellence and was informed by personal communication with Dr. China Billotte Verhoff and Dr. Lindsay Dhanani. This assignment involves asking students to reflect on course topics, their prior knowledge, and potential needs, and to communicate these via anonymous survey responses.

SURVEY

I'm looking forward to having you in class and know that we will all benefit from your contributions. It is important to me that we create a classroom environment that empowers us to have effective conversations that can be difficult.

All of us will have a connection to the topics we are discussing, as we may have had experiences that directly relate to our readings and discussions, or we may have friends or other loved ones who have been impacted by these topics. Part of what we will work on together is how we can have these discussions in a way that promotes our learning. This will include connecting you to resources both on and off campus that can provide you with the support you deserve throughout your academic and professional careers.

I hope we can encourage one another as members of our classroom community to discuss these very important topics. Please come and talk with me at any point if you have questions, concerns, or feedback about how we are navigating these topics.

This survey will help me understand what you may want or require from me and your peers as we begin this journey together. This survey is optional and anonymous.

1. For which of the following course topics would you appreciate resources or conversation? *(Include topics that you will discuss and exclude topics that will not be addressed.)*
    - Ableism
    - Body image
    - Classism
    - Intolerance, prejudice, or bias toward the 2SLGBTQ+ community

- Interpersonal violence
- Racism
- Religious discrimination and intolerance
- Reproductive issues
- Sexism
- Suicidality and/or self-harm
- War
- Xenophobia

2. As each of you will bring new ideas, and new events may occur that need to be addressed, I cannot predict all the organic conversations that we will have as a class. Are there additional areas of discussion that you think may occur in which you would like support or connection to resources? If yes, please explain what type of support or connection would be helpful to you.
3. As your facilitator, I can commit to providing the following: *(List the resources and support you can offer.)*

   - An overview of the readings before you read them so you may know the topics and level of detail you may expect to see
   - A break during class when we are covering these topics
   - Examples of mindfulness activities that will help skill development
   - Flexibility in assignments, attendance, and in how you demonstrate participation
   - A respectful tone
   - Co-creation of community guidelines
   - Demonstration of effective conversations
   - Information about on-campus and off-campus resources

4. What else do you hope I can do to support our classroom community in engaging with these topics? *(If you receive requests that you cannot accommodate, it is helpful to be transparent with students as to why.)*
5. If there are any hopes that you have for your peers in how they engage with the material in this course, or words of support you would like to offer your peers about how you hope to engage with this material, please add them below. I may share what you write with the class.

What Makes This Assignment Culturally Affirming and Meaningful?

By using this optional, anonymous survey, instructors can recognize and value their students' diverse experiences, commit to providing appropriate support, and enter conversations with their students about emotional self-regulation more easily because they have built better rapport. It also helps students consider other perspectives, even if they have not been personally impacted by these topics.

Example 2: Your Story by Emily Murai

Name of Course: College 101: Freshman Seminar

PURPOSE

- To generate insights about one's identity, values, and what shapes and motivates actions and decisions.
- To foster connections with peers.

TASK

This project was modeled on two well-known oral history undertakings, StoryCorps (https://storycorps.org) and Humans of New York (www.humansofnewyork.com). This assignment involves each student writing a story about a meaningful and impactful event in their life and reflecting on how this event had larger implications for their overall story. Student stories will be shared through peer review, oral presentations, in the university's archive, and at a voluntary college-wide open mic at the end of the quarter. The university's stories archive is available to all students, including future cohorts of first-year students who can hear the stories of the students who came before them.

Because stories are a form of narrative characterized by specific structural elements, they illuminate the narrator's attitudes, beliefs, perspectives, and viewpoints, ideally entail struggle, are rich in detail, and shed light on a larger point or issue. To achieve these elements, the assignment stages follow three of Rosenwasser and Stephen's (2018) analytical moves.

Moves One and Two: "Suspend Judgment" and "Notice, Focus and Rank" Read, annotate, and draw inspiration from the assigned readings. Then, step back and observe your life. Brainstorm a list of potential topics or issues that you connect with and that manifest themselves in some form in your own life. Rank the top three or four that most stand out to you and do some exploratory free-writing around them.

Move Three: "Make the Implicit Explicit. Push Observations to Implications by Asking, 'So What?'" Write a four- to five-page (double-spaced) draft about one of the experiences or observations you identified. As you write, keep in mind the four questions Rosenwasser and Stephen (2018) provided to help us think about the larger significance of our story:

- What does the observation imply?
- Why does this observation matter?

- Where does this observation get us?
- How can we begin to theorize the significance of this observation?

Next Steps: Editing and Submitting Your Story   After receiving peer suggestions on your draft, revise and edit the written version of your story. Then, practice reading it aloud. You will be asked to share both the written narrative and a recording of yourself reading the story on the university's stories archive.

What Makes This Assignment Culturally Affirming and Meaningful?

This assignment is culturally affirming because it taps into students' rich, varied cultural backgrounds and allows them to reflect upon their lived experiences in a way that makes sense to them while also teaching valuable writing and analytical skills. In their narratives, students reveal experiences that have helped shape their identities. The assignment gives students an opportunity to reflect upon and tell their stories and think critically about moments when they have (or have not) received support for their cultural identities and lived experiences. Peer reviews, oral presentations, and the archive allow the writer to share these stories with audiences who may be different from them. As Arend and Carlson note in Chapter 3, sharing assignment products with others is an important way to make assignments more meaningful. And, as Martin emphasizes in Chapter 2, this type of assignment is culturally affirming because it can raise the level of connection and cultural awareness among students and in the classroom overall. It is meaningful for other students to listen to their peers' stories and learn about lived experiences that may be very different from their own. They also learn how to build connections across social differences.

Students find it meaningful to go through the process of documenting and analyzing an important experience or realization they have had in their life. Hearing each other's deeply personal stories can strengthen peer relationships, reduce feelings of isolation and loneliness, and empower students and their peers to come together to take collective action around issues of importance to them.

Example 3: Personal Artifacts by Camille Locklear Goins

Name of Course: Supervision and Instructional Leadership

PURPOSE

- To help students connect with one another and their instructor.

- To explore connections between personal experiences and leadership styles.

TASK

This activity was adapted from the Global Oneness Project (www.globalonenessproject.org/stories/student-project-artifacts-our-lives).

After completing the assigned readings, students will identify an artifact that communicates one of their leadership and cultural values. Using Flipgrid, a video recording tool, students will respond to the following questions to the extent they feel comfortable doing so:

- What artifact have you chosen and why?
- What does this artifact tell us about you, your family, your community, your culture, and your leadership values?
- In what ways does the artifact connect to the people in your life personally and professionally?
- What do you want others to know and value about you?
- How will your personal values and experiences influence your administrative philosophy and actions you may take or may make as a school leader?

What Makes This Assignment Culturally Affirming and Meaningful?

School leaders must recognize their own multiple identities, including values shaped by historical, cultural, and familial heritage, and the impact of these identities on their administrative philosophy. Hammond (2015, p. 22) stated, "Culture is the way that every brain makes sense of the world." Culture, therefore, guides individual educational philosophies and has a significant impact on the supervision of instruction and instructional improvement efforts. The examination of personal artifacts allows aspiring school leaders to make connections between their traditions and views of the world and their professional identities and values.

This assignment provides students with an opportunity to share their values and experiences as they begin to craft their administrative philosophy. Through this assignment, students are encouraged to reflect on how their culture is influential in their role as aspiring educational leaders and the decisions they may make. The process of sharing opens a meaningful discussion with peers on how culture influences the learning experience for students.

This assignment personalizes the learning experience, allowing students to make connections between their personal and professional beliefs and values. Students are encouraged to expand on the assignment by designing a plan for working with faculty, students, and families who may have similar or different values.

Example 4: Create Your Own Pride Flag by Kelsie Potter

Name of Course: Introduction to the University: Navigating Pride

PURPOSE

- To increase student knowledge of historical events related to the LGBTQIA+ community and the meaning of the Pride flag.
- To explore and share one's own identities.

TASK

For the instructor   Provide students with a historical context of Pride flags and their role in the movement for Queer/LGBTQIA+ visibility and liberation. This can be in the form of videos, textual materials, documentaries, and so forth. Show students the many examples of Pride flags that represent various identities, such as lesbian, transgender, and bisexual. Point out to students how color and symbols have been used in the flags and how these represent or tie into the identity that is being represented. To remove cost burdens, bring creative materials that students can use to design their own flags during class or have students use technology tools. Consider creating your own flag to share as an example.

For students   During class, students will use the materials to create a Pride flag that represents them and their identities. Students can be encouraged to think about why the rainbow Pride flag was created and what the colors represent before determining what colors or symbols they will use to represent themselves and their identities. Students will also be encouraged to share their rationale for their choices.

Instructors can ask students if they would like to share their flag with the class. Once students who are comfortable sharing have finished, instructors can lead a whole-class discussion using question prompts such as:

- What themes, if any, emerged among the flags?
- Why are Pride flags or identity flags important?
- How did this activity make you think about your identity and the identities of others?

What Makes This Assignment Culturally Affirming and Meaningful?

This activity allows students to think critically about the history of Pride and how the rainbow (among other Pride flags) has become associated with LGBTQIA+ or queer movements. It allows students, especially those who identify as queer, to explore their own identity and how it is situated in the context of Pride. It invites students to feel pride in their identities and their unique circumstances while reaffirming intersectionality and the importance of community development. The discussion questions also require the students to consider group and community identity and how communities or groups came to "adopt" a symbol. Additionally, the inclusion of the instructor participating and sharing their flag as an example can help break barriers between instructors and students and work to remove power dynamics.

This assignment can build authenticity and trust in the classroom, which is especially important when working with LGBTQIA+ students.

Example 5: Life Story by Scott Mattingly and Nadia Bhuiyan

Name of Course: Pursuing Good Work

PURPOSE

- To help students reflect on and articulate their identity and purpose, drawing upon key events and experiences in their lives.
- To enhance the rapport between instructors and students, and hence the students' sense of belonging.

TASK

This assignment is a modified version of McAdams and Guo's (2014) "Life Story Interview." After relating the Life Story concept to prior readings and activities pertaining to personal and social identity as well as purpose, each student is asked to reflect on their life, to date, as if it were a story. More specifically, students are asked to:

1 divide their life story into three central chapters and name them;
2 identify and describe key scenes from their lives;
3 consider and describe the future direction of their lives;
4 identify and describe a life challenge or obstacle that they have encountered and how they have worked to address it;
5 identify and describe something they are particularly proud of doing or accomplishing;
6 identify and describe their values and beliefs, how they came to be, and their single most important value; and
7 identify their life theme.

Instructors can use their discretion in setting expectations for length and structure that are appropriate for their classroom community, but the chief areas of emphasis should be depth of thought and personal relevance.

What Makes This Assignment Culturally Affirming and Meaningful?

This assignment makes space for students to reflect on the events and experiences of their lives in a way that supports a deeper understanding of who they are, what they value, and what they aspire to do. It also supports an improved sense of belonging and rapport between instructors and students. In Chapter 4, Strickland-Davis and McMican emphasize the importance of instructors getting to know their students to develop culturally affirming assignments, and this type of assignment can provide instructors with an in-depth understanding of the assets students bring to the classroom as well as their aspirations. It also serves as an important foundation for future in-class conversations, as students come to understand how their own stories relate to those of others.

Science and Allied Health

Example 6: Reflections and Connections by Caralyn Zehnder

Name of Course: Introductory Biology for Non-Majors

PURPOSE

- To make connections between science concepts and lived experiences for improved understanding of course content.
- To foster self-reflection and regulation skill development.

TASK

Students submit weekly Reflections and Connection journals, in which they reflect on the week's material and connect it to their own lives. Examples of weekly prompts are as follows:

Reflections and Connections 1: Create and then annotate a picture that includes you or a representation of you, showing how you take part in the carbon cycle. Label the processes that move carbon around and the places where carbon is stored.
Reflections and Connections 2: Race, as we know, has no deterministic, biological basis. All the same, race can influence our lives in powerful ways. Explain both sentences using evidence from class and your personal, lived experiences. Include your sources. You can list yourself as a source and you can also use the resources posted for this week.
Reflections and Connections 3: Find a news article that (1) is of interest to you, (2) is about some aspect of biology that we have discussed during the last two weeks, (3) was published in the last two months, and (4) is

more than four paragraphs long. Summarize, analyze, and connect the article to the class using the following format:

- Paragraph 1: Summarize the article in your own words and state its major claim.
- Paragraph 2: Critically evaluate the article by answering the following three questions:
  - What evidence is provided in the article in support of the major claim?
  - How reliable is the evidence?
  - What bias may be influencing the claim?
- Paragraph 3: Describe how this article connects to something you learned in this course within the past two weeks.
- Article citation: Include the article title and a link to the article.

Reflections and Connections 4: What has been the most interesting or important idea that you have learned in this course so far? How might understanding this concept help you in your future coursework, career, or personal life? What is something you are curious about regarding this topic or something about this topic that you would like to share?

What Makes This Assignment Culturally Affirming and Meaningful?

Reflections and Connections is a culturally affirming assignment because it allows for co-constructions of knowledge by students and integrates students' lived experiences with course content, the assignment description is transparent, and writing mechanics are not weighed heavily (Zehnder et al., 2021). This assignment is not based on students recalling information from lectures, so their responses are not constrained by didactic instruction. Instead, it asks students to reflect on how the biology course content is connected to important societal questions. There are no "right" or "wrong" answers; instead, students reflect on meaningful connections between the course content and their lives. Their lived experiences are a valuable resource, and this assignment allows them to bring this part of themselves into a biology course. The resources that accompany each prompt are carefully selected to include diverse viewpoints, especially from people who have been traditionally excluded from scientific discourse.

The full assignment description follows the TILT framework (Winkelmes et al., 2016), clearly stating the assignment's purpose, how completing it will benefit students, the steps students need to take to complete it, and the grading rubric with annotated examples. Following the TILT framework uncovers the "hidden curriculum" that obfuscates learning in many assignments and prevents all students from participating fully in the learning opportunity. The grading rubric for this assignment emphasizes individual connections and thoughts over writing mechanics. If writing quality were more heavily emphasized, this assignment would likely induce anxiety among many students, especially as there is no formal writing instruction in this course.

Reflections and Connections is meaningful because students connect course content to important societal issues that directly impact their lives. Many of the Reflections and Connections prompts include a social justice perspective, which is meaningful for many students.

Example 7: Exploring Favorite Foods by Judy C. K. Chan

Name of Course: Exploring Our Foods: An Introduction to Food Science

PURPOSE

- To increase knowledge about processed foods so that more informed choices about food can be made.

TASK

Part I For this assignment, students take a photo of a processed food item in their pantry or refrigerator or find a picture online. Students then upload the picture to the online small group discussion board and briefly describe (in about 100 words) why they picked this particular food and why it is important to their everyday diet and life. They should also indicate how their cultural value, family upbringing, or simply conversations they have had with their friends and relatives affected their choice. Next, students list five scientific questions they have about this food (see syllabus for examples and inspiration).

Part II Students work with their assigned group members to investigate the scientific questions posed about the foods in the first part of the assignment. This is a team-based research assignment where group team members will research the ingredients used in the identified foods and answer the questions posed.

What Makes This Assignment Culturally Affirming and Meaningful?

Food serves as a community-building tool, and this personalized small group assignment on food preferences enables students to approach the chemistry, microbiology, and laws and regulations of foods in a personally meaningful and collaborative way. By inviting students to select their favorite processed foods, they are immediately able to see the relevance of what is being learned. This assignment also gives space for students to show off and celebrate their cultural foods. It is quite impactful to see a discussion board full of photos of kimchi, dried anchovy, ketchup, tofu, masala-flavored potato chips, pepperoni, and so forth. When students identify similar food products, this helps them foster connections with one another. Students will often share comments such as "I ate that as a kid too!" or "Where do you get this food around campus?" Working in small groups enables students to learn more about each other as they also dive into the content of the course.

Example 8: Formal Letter to Elected Official by Shalini Srinivasan

Name of Course: Principles of Chemistry

PURPOSE

- To develop knowledge of how science, technology, engineering, art, and math issues impact communities and the world.
- To develop an academic voice and write persuasively.

TASK

Students are asked to write a letter to an elected official about a STEM or STEAM issue that they care about and that is impacting their community, city, state, or the world at large. Students can choose to write letters about a broad range of topics. To write the letter, students need to engage in research about their communities and their identified issues. Although students do not have to mail their letters, this type of assignment can initiate civic engagement.

What Makes This Assignment Culturally Affirming and Meaningful?

This assignment builds bridges of relevance between home, community, and classroom experiences (see Chapter 2). It also gives students the space and freedom to produce a document that uniquely represents their attitudes, while simultaneously encouraging an evidence-based approach to making their arguments.

The assignment does not limit the scope of topics that students can select and discuss in their letters. Choice in assignments is culturally affirming (see Chapter 6). Although students are not required to mail their letters, Arend and Carlson (Chapter 3) point out that even a pretend audience can increase the authenticity and meaningfulness of an assignment. This assignment also gives each student a platform to share their voice, which can be especially important for students from historically and currently underserved groups.

Example 9: Culture and Healthcare by Fathia Richardson and Kathleen Polimeni

Name of Course: Global Health and Diversity in Nursing

PURPOSE

- To understand how healthcare systems and practices vary across cultures and countries.
- To discover the importance of nurses considering cultural factors when supporting and treating patients.

TASK

For this assignment, students work in a small group to research healthcare practices and policies of a country of their choice and then create a presentation to share what they learned with their classmates. The presentations should include cultural and religious beliefs related to healthcare, economic and political policies and practices, access to healthcare, vulnerable populations, diseases most likely to impact those living in this country or from this cultural background, healthcare prevention strategies, and the role of the nurse. Before formally presenting to the class, each group will do a practice session with another group, with the two groups then providing feedback to each other. On the day when all groups formally present what they have learned, students in the audience will be asked to identify similarities and differences between their country and those in the other presentations. These discoveries will be documented in a matrix and submitted as part of the assignment. The final part of the assignment is a reflection paper where students will discuss why it is important for nurses to consider the cultural identities of their patients.

What Makes This Assignment Culturally Affirming and Meaningful?

This assignment encourages students to consider how cultural factors influence how healthcare is practiced in other countries and why nurses need to consider cultural factors when practicing. The presentation component of the assignment enables students to learn from one another and discover similarities and differences in healthcare practices across different cultures. It is meaningful because students are explicitly asked to reflect on why nurses need to be culturally competent and consider cultural factors when treating patients.

Arts and Humanities

Example 10: Empowering Ideas: Philosophy Dialogue Project by Wendy L. Ostroff

Name of Course: Exploring the Unknown

PURPOSE

- To explore diverse perspectives and how ideas are developed and used.

TASK

As the author of *The Deepest Human Life* wrote, "all ideas under philosophical discussion, in the end, must be judged on their ability to help us live well" (Samuelson, 2014, p. 10). Many people who have impacted the way we think and live our lives (e.g., Ban Zhou, Virginia Woolf, Toni Morrison, Jesus) never considered themselves philosophers; yet, their ideas can be powerful, especially when we are in need of uplifting or consoling.

Part 1: Research   After reading Scott Samuelson's *The Deepest Human Life* and Buxton & Whiting's *The Philosopher Queens: The Lives and Legacies of Philosophy's Unsung Women*, students will choose a philosopher to research. Each student will need to choose a different philosopher and is encouraged to consider philosophers from non-Western, non-dominant groups.

Each student will need to locate and read at least one primary text written by their chosen philosopher and select several key passages that exemplify the philosopher's views on life. They are encouraged to choose provocative passages and that will lead to a spirited discussion of the philosopher's ideas. They will need to gather at least three additional scholarly resources to learn more about the philosopher. This assignment focuses on the evolution and development of philosophers' ideas and the students' interpretation of how those ideas can be applied; it is not a biographical exercise.

Each student will investigate the following:

- What is the philosopher's intellectual work and how has it evolved?
- How was their work received or interpreted by the public, including by different groups of people with various identities?
- How was the work initially interpreted, and how has that changed over time?
- How has the philosopher been understood or misunderstood?

Part 2: In-Class Dialogue Each student will lead a 15-minute in-class dialogue on their philosopher's ideas. They will share the key passages they identified with their classmates, who should read these prior to the discussion. During the discussion, the student will situate the passages into the broader context of the philosopher's work and inform the class how these passages represent the questions and issues that the philosopher addressed. Next, they will share discussion prompts that will facilitate the dialogue.

What Makes This Assignment Culturally Affirming and Meaningful?

This assignment widens students' views of who is a philosopher and who has been able to claim that title throughout history. It challenges the notion that philosophy is an elite category of thought and encourages students to take both others' and their own ideas seriously. As Martin advocates in Chapter 2, this assignment encourages students to explore diverse perspectives rather than rely on voices from the Western, dominant culture. The dialogue part of the assignment further illuminates the concept that all voices are valuable.

Example 11: Oral History Project by Meredith May

Name of Course: United States History since 1877

PURPOSE

- To explore individual experiences and perspectives related to historical events and how these events impact people differently.

TASK

This project involves students conducting an oral history interview and then documenting what was learned. The final product will be archived at a local historical museum so students will be making a major contribution to the recording of local history.

Each student will be assigned a partner and an interviewee. The interviews can take place at the person's assisted living center, the historical museum, the college, or the public library. During the interview, students will ask a series of questions to learn about the person's life and how historical events impacted them personally. Two critical questions will drive the conversation:

- What can one person's story tell us about big historical forces?
- How do the decisions made by historical figures, such as presidents and other leaders, impact "ordinary" people?

Students will evaluate the importance of individual accounts in the study of larger historical events, taking one person's experiences and comparing them to the broader context. For example, if the students interview someone who worked in the local oil industry, they would compare the interviewee's experiences to what they have discovered about the broader history of oil in Texas and the United States through research.

Although two students will conduct the interview together, each student will write their own paper about the interview and what they learned. Students are expected to explore the historical issues through research in addition to conducting the interview. Sources should be documented using MLA in-text citations and in a works-cited page. The final document should be at least 1,000 words in length.

An introductory paragraph or two will highlight the main historical themes that will be addressed in the rest of the paper (e.g., Civil Rights, 1950s culture, cultural change in the 1960s and 1970s, feminism, stagflation, Vietnam, Reagan). This should include a thesis statement that states if the interviewee's experiences represent the major themes of certain eras.

The second part of the paper comprises a biographical sketch that should include details of the interviewee's age, where they have lived, family roles, class, race, ethnicity, religion, and other aspects of their identity, education, occupations, military service (if applicable), and any other information that the student deems important in establishing the interviewee's contexts and perspectives.

Next, the paper will dive into the interviewee's experiences and compare them to what the student learned from secondary sources. This section might consist of more than one paragraph.

In the conclusion, the student should reflect on what they have learned not only from the interviewee but also about the process of conducting research that combines an oral interview with other traditional research methods.

Finally, the student should list all the sources they consulted in a works-cited page.

Formative assessments will enable students to complete the steps of the project in sequence and receive feedback as they progress. Students will be asked to watch instructional videos and engage in an online discussion about planning the project. They will then need to confirm that they have scheduled the interview and drafted a timetable that will enable them to complete the assignment in a timely manner. Next, they will post updates on their projects on an online discussion board. Finally, they will submit their final papers.

What Makes This Assignment Culturally Affirming and Meaningful?

All too often, history is presented to students as something that happens in "other places" to people far away and long ago. It is often depicted in a very static manner and students may perceive the primary goal as merely memorizing facts. By contrast, this assignment personalizes local history and shows students that history happens to everyone and in their own backyard. Additionally, part of their analysis will show that historical events happen to different people in different ways. A person's physical location, cultural heritage, gender, socio-economic status, age, and many other factors will skew how historical events are both perceived and experienced. Students will discover that asking five neighbors how they experienced the economic shifts of the 1970s will likely result in five very different answers, even though they all lived through the same period.

In the classroom discussions before the assignment, students will discuss whose voices and perspectives are typically captured in historical records and whose are often excluded. They will learn how historians must often read against the grain to hear the voices of those who are rarely included. They will find this meaningful because, rather than writing only for their instructor, they will contribute to the historical record by creating an archival resource that adds more voices to the past and paints a more complete picture of history. They get to do more than merely study the past; they contribute a lasting piece of it.

Example 12: We Poems: Collective Voices Speak Individual Truths by Portia Scott

Name of Course: English/Composition

PURPOSE

- To explore students' own identities while learning how to write poems.

TASK

Students will listen to "We Real Cool" by Gwendolyn Brooks (www.youtube.com/watch?v=oaVfLwZ6jes) and then use it as a model to write their own personalized expression of "we." The first two lines, like Brooks's, will show character and setting, which is where students indicate early personalization. Each student's poem must have an end rhyme ("we"), an internal rhyme as couplets, as in "We Real Cool," and an expression and explanation of how they see themselves. The finished poems should have the same number of lines (ten) as Brooks's work.

What Makes This Assignment Culturally Affirming and Meaningful?

An important aspect of this assignment being culturally affirming is Gwendolyn Brooks herself. In 1950, she was the first African American to win the Pulitzer Prize. Having students write about themselves adds meaning to the assignment. They will feel empowered as they demonstrate learning related to literary elements while being represented authentically.

In previous submissions, students will have written about an individual cultural trait or, in some cases, provided insightful, in-depth descriptions of intersectionality. In Brooks's own words during an interview about "We Real Cool," she expressed her desire to focus on what individuals thought about themselves. Students of color regularly embark on the dual existence of being thrust into a sphere formed by environmental constraints of whom and what others think they are. This assignment frees them to define an existence for themselves.

Example 13: Who We Are: Memoir Reading, Writing, and Sharing by Lorraine Cella

Name of Course: Writing/Composition

PURPOSE

- To explore and evaluate memoirs written by diverse authors.
- To write a personal memoir that helps students get to know one another and practice writing skills.

TASK

Part 1: Read and Analyze Memoirs   After learning about various types of memoir and collectively analyzing Lauren Mauldin's "The Colors of His Addiction," including discussing the writer's purpose, style, and, sadly, the universality of drug addiction, students will review a variety of short memoirs from a diverse group of current writers and then respond to question prompts. Each student can choose to work independently or with a partner, and they must respond to the following questions about at least four memoirs they select:

- What does it say?
- What does it mean?
- Why does it matter?
- What writing techniques are effective?

Sample memoirs:

- Memoir of Object/Possession/Artifact:
    - "Barbie-Q" by Sandra Cisneros

- "My Young Mind Was Disturbed by a Book. It Changed My Life" by Viet Thanh Nguyen
- Memoir of Event or Situation:
  - Excerpt from *In My Skin: My Life on and off the Basketball Court* by Brittney Griner
  - "Harvey Weinstein Is My Monster, Too" by Salma Hayek
  - Excerpt from *I Am Malala* by Malala Yousafzai
- Memoir of Person:
  - "All Parents Are Cowards" by Michael Christie
  - "I Fit the Description" by Steve Locke
  - "How Do We Forgive Our Fathers?" by Dick Lourie, adapted by Sherman Alexie
- Memoir of Place:
  - Excerpt from *Decoded* by Jay-Z
  - "Fish Cheeks" by Amy Tan
- Memoir of Observation:
  - "Cruel as It Is, We Somehow Go on" by Leonard Pitts
  - "Bringing Parents up to Code" by Rick Reilly

Part 2: Compose Stories and Share Next, students will write their own memoirs. These can be in any format, including creative non-fiction, poem, letter, diary, journal entry, or infographic. Students are also invited to identify alternative formats. They must post an excerpt for the class and the entire piece for the instructor.

What Makes This Assignment Culturally Affirming and Meaningful?

As a first assignment, the playing field is level because students draw from their own lives—everyone has something to say, ideas to share, and stories to tell. This assignment builds a community of learners. Diverse perspectives are shared via the list of memoir options. Students get to learn about each other and welcome one another to the course. This assignment also serves to honor each student, their history, and their identities.

As George and Thompson point out in Chapter 6, product and process choices affirm students. In this assignment, students can share their stories in diverse ways; and they can choose to work independently or with a partner during the first part, which enables them to take ownership of the learning experience.

***Example 14: Exploring Fascism in Spain* by Lunden E. MacDonald**

Name of Course: Culture and Civilization of Spain

PURPOSE

- To learn about various perspectives on fascism in Spain.

TASK

Pre-work   Students participate in an introductory lecture on pre-Civil War Spain, complete assigned readings that represent diverse voices, watch a video, and reflect on what was learned by answering the following questions:

- What did you know about fascism and the Franco dictatorship in Spain before completing this pre-work? Feel free to include anything, from historical facts to personal opinions or preconceived notions.
- What questions remain unanswered for you, or what is unclear about the material we covered today?
- What would you like to learn more about? How can you plan to learn more?

Part I: Concept Mapping   Students work with their assigned small groups to create a concept map that details the salient points of the lecture and the readings.

Part II: Online Discussion   For the initial post, in about 500 words students share at least one connection (e.g., connecting self-to-text, self-to-self, or self-to-other) they made to what they learned about fascism, citing sources. They are encouraged to include explicit commentary on how their cultural background or experiences inform their understanding of history. For the second part of the discussion, students will ask at least two questions of their peers about their initial post; and for the final part, they will answer at least two questions posed by their peers.

What Makes This Assignment Culturally Affirming and Meaningful?

This assignment requires students to comment on how their cultural background and experiences inform their learning. As Martin advocates in Chapter 2, all students are invited to bring their perspective and cultural capital to the table and share it with others. The whole-class discussion encourages relationship-building within the classroom community and also, via empathy, with the larger imagined communities with which the students interact every day.

The assignment fosters respectful, empathetic, and collaborative discussion of difficult topics, such as contemporary politics in the United States. Students often comment on how it engages their civic responsibility by encouraging them to vote, if they can, or engage in election-related activism and illuminates the importance of learning and affirming the socio-political circumstances of different cultural groups throughout history. Finally, it dispels previously held myths and misconceptions and provides a new perspective on colonialism and its long-term effects. By aligning the assignment to the overall learning outcomes of the course, students understand that the course is not limited to a content-focused and unilateral review of historical dates and characters but instead creates space for culture, both historical and contemporary, to impact real-time learning and individualized personal growth.

Example 15: A Collaborative Diversity, Equity, Inclusion, and Access (DEIA) Student Poster by Marie-Therese C. Sulit and Charles Zola

Name of Course: The Moral of the Story, an Honors Interdisciplinary Seminar

PURPOSE

- To explore how diversity, equity, inclusion, and access (DEIA) issues are communicated in various types of literature.
- To discuss how literature can be used to promote DEIA.

TASK

Working collaboratively in a small group, students will create a poster on DEIA topics and issues related to course readings. The final posters will be presented at a campus-wide symposium at the end of the term. After reading classic and Western-oriented, contemporary, non-Western, and underrepresented literary pieces, students will identify DEIA themes that emerged across the readings and quotes from each piece related to the identified themes. At the poster session, students will summarize the DEIA themes they discovered in the literature they reviewed and share ideas about how literature can be used to advance DEIA issues.

What Makes This Assignment Culturally Affirming and Meaningful?

This assignment has an intentional focus on DEIA and how these issues are addressed in various types of literature. Students can use their varied cultural identities and lived experiences to determine the DEIA themes that were evidenced in the assigned literature. As suggested by Martin in Chapter 2, the assigned readings are carefully selected to ensure diverse approaches and perspectives.

Education

Example 16: Identity and Intersectionality Personal and Leadership Reflection by Theresa Haug-Belvin

Name of Course: Leader: Teacher & Mentor

PURPOSE

- To reflect on one's own identities and how they intersect, and how these identities and related experiences may be similar to or different from those of others, including students.
- To determine how reflecting on identity can strengthen leadership skills as an educator.

TASK

This activity and the related assignment were adapted from www.teampedia.net/wiki/Forced_Choice and require approximately 30–60 minutes of class time before students complete the written part of the assignment. To prepare for this activity, instructors will need to write the following on large sticky sheets that are then placed around the room:

- race
- ethnicity
- sexual orientation
- immigration status
- body size/shape
- ability
- socio-economic status
- education
- age

Students can then be invited to suggest further identities, which the instructor should again write on large sticky sheets and hang around the room.

Activity Introduction All of us have multiple, intersecting identities that make our experiences different from those of people around us. This activity will allow you the space to consider which identity you most identify with in different situations. You can also observe your classmates doing the same. Pay attention to which identities you and your classmates select, and use this activity to get to know more about yourself and others.

After I read a statement, find the identity hanging on the wall that you most identify with in that situation and stand by the identity sheet. Once everyone has selected their identity, if you wish to share with the class why you chose that identity, you are welcome to do so. At no point will you be expected to contribute, so only do so if you want to.

The Statements

- This is the identity I am most aware of at home.
- This is the identity I am most aware of at school/work.
- This is the identity I know the most about.
- This is the identity I know the least about.
- This is the identity I tend to keep hidden.
- This is the identity I most like to share with others.
- This is the identity I am most unsure of how to talk about.
- This is the identity that I think most people judge me by.
- This is the identity that brings me the most happiness.
- This is the identity that brings me the most pain.
- This is the identity that is most important to me.

Written Reflection Paper Students will write a reflection paper about their experience participating in this activity, commenting on what they learned about themselves and their classmates. Next, they will write about how their identities and the intersectionality of these identities can impact the actions they take as a leader. In addition, they will comment on how reflecting on their identities and the identities of others can help them be more effective leaders and educators. Throughout the paper, students should make connections to the readings, especially those relating to leadership styles and approaches.

What Makes This Assignment Culturally Affirming and Meaningful?

This assignment provides students with the space to consider their various identities and how these identities might be similar to or different from those of others. The written reflection paper also requires students to consider how the intersectionality of their identities may impact their leadership style and actions. In Chapter 2, Martin encourages instructors to give students opportunities to consider and reflect on how culture and identity influence experiences. Providing students with a safe space in which to voice their experiences can be particularly uplifting, not only for the individual but for the class as a whole.

Example 17: Language History Project by Laura Alvarez and Sarah Capitelli

Name of Course: Teaching Multilingual Students

PURPOSE

- To explore how language plays a key role in one's identity and lived experiences within and outside schools.
- To determine ways to honor, value, and support multilingual students and families as an educator.

TASK

Part 1: Self-Reflection on Language   After students engage with poems, spoken word, visual pieces, and graphic novels in which different authors explore their language histories, they are asked to choose a modality to share their experiences creatively as users and learners of the language. In the past, students have created drawings, slideshows, poems, graphic novels or comic strips, children's books, collages, maps, timelines, videos, and podcasts.

Students can use the following question prompts to spur their reflection on their language history:

- How have languages been lost or maintained in your family history through immigration, marriage, conquests, colonization, school, and so forth?
- What languages, language practices, or dialects did you grow up with?
- How have you learned languages (e.g., from particular family members, school, travel or living in another country, work, or friendships)?
- How do you use your languages with different people in your life and/or for different purposes?
- How is language part of your identity?
- What feelings, values, or beliefs do you have about your languages?
- What feelings, values, and/or beliefs did your family communicate to you about language?
- How has language made you feel like you do or do not belong somewhere?

Rather than respond to all the questions, students should focus on those that are most relevant to their own lives. Each student is asked to bring their reflection piece to the next class session and share it with their classmates in a gallery walk and in small groups. The class then discusses commonalities and differences and what they are taking away from the experience about how language matters in people's lives and the implications for their role as future educators of linguistically diverse learners.

Part 2: Application Reflection   Students are then asked to write a reflection piece about what they learned from participating in this experience and how it will help them become better educators. They are encouraged to think about ways that they can honor and value the multilingual aspects of their students' identities. In their written reflection, students are required to draw on articles or other materials they have engaged with in the course so far.

What Makes This Assignment Culturally Affirming and Meaningful?

The assignment is culturally affirming because it grounds the study of language in students' own experiences. By centering the conversation on their experiences, students take away crucial insights about the relationship between language and culture, and how language practices are a key aspect of identity. Students who come from bi/multilingual homes often reflect on the value of their home language. During the activity and subsequent conversation, students reflect on the role schools have played in linguistic and cultural erasure in U.S. history, which is a common theme in many students' histories. As a result of this experience, students reflect on how they will intentionally strive to create culturally and linguistically sustaining classrooms for their own K-12 students.

In addition, the activities and conversations help build relationships and a sense of community at the beginning of the semester, which creates a foundation for learning throughout the term (see Chapter 4). Through the different phases of the assignment, the activities serve to decenter English monolingualism and highlight the value of students' home languages.

Another key reason why this assignment is culturally affirming and meaningful is that students can choose how they would like to communicate ideas relating to the exercise. In Chapter 6, George and Thompson highlight how choice provides an opportunity to build on student strengths.

Example 18: Reclaiming Numbers and Healing from White Supremacy Culture by Diana Recouvreur

Name of Course: Quantitative Methods for Social Justice Inquiry

PURPOSE

- To heal from the educational harm of traditional math education.
- To practice asset-based approaches to data interpretation.

TASK

Before each class, students are given a reflection prompt to consider. They need to come to class prepared to discuss their responses during the community check-in that takes place during the first part of the class. The question prompts relate to the readings and weekly topics that are addressed in class. Each prompt is explicitly healing-centered at first (Garcia et al., 2023), then shifts to applying the following tenets of QuantCrit (Gillborn et al., 2018):

1. The centrality of racism is a complex and deeply rooted aspect of society that is not readily amenable to quantification.
2. Numbers are not neutral and should be interrogated for their role in promoting deficit analyses that serve White racial interests.
3. Categories are neither natural nor given, so the units and forms of analysis must be critically evaluated.
4. Voice and insight are vital; data cannot speak for itself and critical analyses should be informed by the experiential knowledge of marginalized groups.
5. Statistical analyses have no inherent value but can play a role in struggles for social justice.

One example of a prompt is as follows:

- How are you doing today?
- After reviewing this week's Reclaiming Numbers article and How to QuantCrit, identify an example of how numbers or data are shared via a deficit frame. What communities or cultures are negatively or positively impacted by the way the data was shared? How would you reframe the data through an asset-based, socially just lens?

What Makes This Assignment Culturally Affirming and Meaningful?

Unfortunately, many students come into class carrying significant math anxiety and avoid quantitative methods in their research. This assignment focuses on the importance of evaluating data via a critical lens. For educational leaders to transform systems, first some healing is needed, followed by reframing of what numbers are and can be. The hope is that continued reflection, dialogue, and affirmation will cultivate more empowering patterns to supplant the oppressive ones. This assignment encourages students to discover and disrupt the problematic ways that numbers and data are still used to pathologize BIPOC communities, and to see numerical data and quantitative methods as tools that can be used to advance social justice.

Example 19: Community Portrait by Brie Morettini

Name of Course: Working with Families and Communities

PURPOSE

- To develop an asset-based, inclusive understanding of how family and community members can support children's educational experiences.
- To develop engagement plans to leverage family and community partnerships aimed at supporting students educationally.

TASK

Part I: Community History and Overview (3–4 Pages) Students should identify a community they can visit frequently. Working in pairs or small groups, students will research demographic information, the history of the community, and current trends or priorities of the community. They will then present their findings in a narrative form. The narrative should capture the everyday experiences of people who live in the community.

Part II: Interviews (3–4 Pages) For this portion of the assignment, students gather information from at least three members of their identified community. These will be individuals who live and—ideally—work in the community. Some examples of potential interviewees are parents/grandparents, guardians, small business owners, teachers, principals, librarians, and postal workers. Students will develop a protocol of approximately five questions to ask the community members relating to their everyday experiences living or working in the community. This should focus on debunking myths and assumptions about the community. Interviews should be recorded and transcribed. Students will then review the transcripts and write a synthesized analysis of the interview data.

Part III: Community Asset Maps (2–3 Pages) When possible, students should use Google Maps to indicate features such as schools, social services sites, residential areas, healthcare institutions, restaurants, shelters, and transportation lines on an aerial map of the identified community. They should then submit this map.

Part IV: Inclusive Engagement Plan (2–3 Pages) Based on the data collected and the assigned readings, students will develop an inclusive engagement plan for families and community members. Each plan should address the following questions:

- What do you know about children's everyday experiences in the community?
- What do you know about children's cultural backgrounds, language practices, and interests?
- How can you work effectively with families and the community to make your classroom a welcoming space?
- How will you, as a teacher, build on children's personal, cultural, and community assets to build a safe and welcoming learning space?

What Makes This Assignment Culturally Affirming and Meaningful?

This assignment is designed to heighten inclusive teacher candidates' awareness of the roles that family and community members have on a child's success in school. It situates students' communities and families from an asset-based perspective, demonstrating that all children must be understood in the context of their community environment, including their families, schools, neighborhoods, and wider society. Students are encouraged to debunk myths or assumptions about family and community members and identify ways to partner with family and community members to support student success in school.

Example 20: Books You Wish You Had Read by Brian Kayser

Name of Course: Cultural Pluralism

PURPOSE

- To analyze instructional materials via a cultural lens.
- To select inclusive course materials that are reflective of a diverse student body.

TASK

In this assignment, students work in groups to research books they wish they had read in K-12. After identifying at least three books, they use a simplified version of Student Achievement Partners' Text Analysis Tool (https://achievethecore.org/page/3369/text-analysis-toolkit), a free resource that helps teachers analyze a book for culturally relevant tenets. After completing this analysis, students explain how the selected books will support students' academic success, build cultural competence, and support students' growth in critical consciousness. Their explanations can be shared with the class via a written product, orally, or using a multimedia approach. Students also post their work on a discussion board and comment on their peers' work.

What Makes This Assignment Culturally Affirming and Meaningful?

As students analyze each book, they become more knowledgeable of texts that perpetuate harmful stereotypes and more adept at reading children's books through a culturally relevant teacher lens. They immediately see the relevance of this task because they know they will need to select books and course materials as a teacher. This assignment is culturally affirming because students can choose any book they like and share the reasons for their selection. It can be modified so that students complete it individually, but as this is a new experience for them, completing it in groups encourages sustained discussion throughout the task. Giving students the freedom to choose from various sharing options also enhances the meaningfulness of the assignment.

References

Garcia, N. M., Vélez, V. N., & Pérez Huber, L. (2023). Can numbers be gender and race-conscious? Advocating for a critical race feminista quantitative praxis in education. *Equity and Excellence in Education*, 56(1/2), 190–205. https://doi.org/10.1080/10665684.2022.2047413.

Gillborn, D., Warmington, P., & Demack, S. (2018). QuantCrit: Education, policy, "Big Data" and principles for a critical race theory of statistics. *Race Ethnicity and Education*, 21(2), 158–179.

Hammond, Z. L. (2015). *Culturally responsive teaching and the brain*. Corwin Press.

McAdams, D. P., & Guo, J. (2014). How shall I live? Constructing a life story in the college years. *New Directions for Higher Education*, 166, 15–23. doi:10.1002/he.20091.

Rosenwasser, D., & Stephen, J. (2018). *Writing analytically* (8th ed.). Cengage Learning.

Samuelson, S. (2014). *The deepest human life: An introduction to philosophy for everyone*. University of Chicago Press.

Winkelmes, M., Bernacki, M., Butler, J., Zochowski, M., Golanics, J., & Weavil, K. H. (2016). A teaching intervention that increases underserved college students' success. *Peer Review; Washington*, 8(1/2), 31–36. https://www.proquest.com/docview/1805184428.

Zehnder, C., Alby, C., Kleine, K., & Metzker, J. (2021). *Learning that matters: A field guide to course design for transformative education*. Myers Education Press.

Index

ADDIE instructional design 17–18
adult learning principles 43
alignment map **41**
alternative assignments 74, 83
analytical reasoning 49
analytical rubric 108–109
andragogy 38, 53
attendance 88, 135
authentic tasks 46
autonomy 45–46, 88, 92–94, 97

background knowledge 116–117
backward design 4, 14–15, 21
bias in testing 72
blogs 5, 78–79
Bloom 15, 75, 106
book reviews 5, 79–80, 83

campus resources 60, 119, 135
career aspirations 48–49, 65
career skills 40, 48–49, 51, 80
checklist, culturally affirming assignments 2
checklist rubric 108
choice, types of 92–98
choice overload 91–92
collaboration 50, 73, 78, 90, 98, 126
college knowledge 103, 111
concept maps 46
constructivism 74
contract grading 96–97
conversational commenting 124–125
creativity 49, 71, 74–75, 95, 108
criterion-referenced grading 89, 90
critical digital pedagogy 79
critical thinking 42, 49–50, 104
cross-cultural competencies 30
cultural capital 24, 152

cultural competence 23, 90, 160
cultural wealth 44
culturally responsive teaching 23
curriculum design 8
curriculum maps 39

diversity audit 56, 58
drafts 82, 106, 126
due dates 67, 93, 97, 121

equity gaps 1, 59, 72, 96
exam 71–75, 92, 96, 116, 122, 127–128
executive summaries 5, 76, 83
expectancy-value model 89
experiential learning 5, 80–81

feedback 18, 26, 28; characteristics of 5, 32, 114–128; peer 5, 77, 125–126
Fink, D. 15, 38, 42, 46
first day of class activities 55, 61
first-generation students 5, 59–60, 103, 111, 115
flexibility 19, 38, 67, 87–88, 92, 95, 135
formative assessment 18, 82, 118–119

grading criteria 107–109, 111
grading policies 18–19
grit 55
growth-focused 40–41, 51, 122
growth mindset 40, 46, 122
guided topic choice 93

holistic rubric 108

identities 11, 23–29, 31–33
imposter syndrome 7, 11, 13, 23
infographic 5, 16, 75–76, 83

instructional design 13–14, 16, 19
instructor–student relationship 55–59
internships 80
intersectionality 29, 140, 150, 154–155
intrinsic motivation 89, 114
invisible curriculum 111

jigsaw classroom 63

Knowles, M. 37–38, 43

late work policies 19
learning outcomes 39–42, 44, 51, 57, 59, 66, 71, 75, 83

metacognition 4, 45, 127–128
models 4, 14, 65–66, 75, 102, 109, 118, 128
multicultural 29, 33
multiple-choice exams 71, 72, 96

NACE competencies **50**

one-pagers 5, 76, 83
online discussions 62, 97, 106
ownership 45, 89, 94–98, 151

Pecha Kucha 5, 62, 76–77, 83
peer-reviewed research 73, 106
persistence rates 55
personalized language 63–64
playbooks 81
podcasts 5, 16, 32, 77, 78, 95
poetry 25, 32, 79, 93
policy briefs 76
positionality 11, 12, 18, 31, 56–57
positive affirmations 66
presentations 20, 76–77
principle, meaningful assignments 37–51, **40**
principles, culturally affirming assignments 24–32, **25**
prior knowledge 40, 43–44, 57, 110
process choice 76, 97
product choice 92, 95
program-level learning outcomes 39, 40, 51
project management 49
pronouns 61, 64–65
pronunciation of students' names 61
public scholarship 78, 79

purpose of the assignment 31, 101, 103, 120

quizzes 39, 41, 82, 92, 106

real-world value 40, 46, 47, 51
reflection 56, 119, 127–128
reflective essay 42
relevance 17, 28, 39, 43, 46–47, 51
research papers 1, 5, 71–75, 95, 96
retention rates 19
rubrics 108, 109, 114–116

scaffolded support 5, 44
screencast 59–60, 78, 117
self-correction 124
self-determination theory 88,
sense of belonging 1, 2, 58, 102, 122
social media 47, 78, 79
socioeconomic mobility 12
standardized tests 83
stereotype threat 72–73, 119, 120
summative assessments 17, 18, 74, 82
survey 58, 116, 119
syllabus 18–20, 48, 59–60, 63, 105, 117

tacit knowledge 114–116, 128
teaching philosophy 18, 56–57, 59, 68
testing bias 72
TILT (Transparency in Learning and Technology) 66, 101, 104–107, 110–111
traditional assignments 1, 5, 72–75, 83, 91
training manuals 5, 81, 83
transferable skills 91
transparency 28, 45, 66, 101–102, **104**, 106–109

Understanding by Design (UbD) 14

VALUE rubric 25, 109
videos 5, 16, 59, 63, 77–78, 95, 106, 116

Winkelmes, M.-A. 66, 101–107, 142

Yosso, T. J. 24, 58, 66, 74

zone of proximal development 44

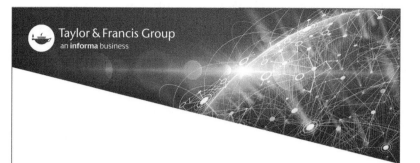